Robert Burns, Andrew Lang

Selected Poems

Robert Burns, Andrew Lang

Selected Poems

ISBN/EAN: 9783744712866

Printed in Europe, USA, Canada, Australia, Japan

Cover: Foto ©Thomas Meinert / pixelio.de

More available books at **www.hansebooks.com**

SELECTED POEMS

OF

ROBERT BURNS

WITH AN INTRODU

ANDREW L

LONDON

KEGAN PAUL, TRENCH, TRÜB

MDCCCXCI

PREFATORY NOTE.

THE text of the Poems in this Selection is in accordance with the earliest texts of Kilmarnock, of Edinburgh, and of the scattered tracts and the additions made by Currie and others. Where Burns originally wrote a coarse line, which he afterwards replaced by another, the second reading is given, as more in harmony with modern taste. The Editor has to thank Mrs. Ogleby, for collating the texts, and Mr. Craibe Angus, for kindly lending examples of early and rare editions. Because these editions are rare, and that the curious may see the text as nearly as possible as the poet saw it, the peculiarities of printing have been preserved.

CONTENTS.

	PAGE
INTRODUCTION	xi

POEMS:—

The Twa Dogs (a Tale)	1
Scotch Drink	11
The Holy Fair	17
The Brigs of Ayr	27
Address to the Deil	37
The Vision	42
Address to the Unco Guid, or the Rigidly Righteous	52
Halloween	55
The Jolly Beggars	66
The Auld Farmer's New-Year Morning Salutation to his Auld Mare, Maggie	81
The Cotter's Saturday Night	86
A Prayer, in the Prospect of Death	94
A Prayer, under the Pressure of Violent Anguish	95
To a Mountain Daisy	96
Epistle to a Young Friend	99
To a Haggis	103
To W*** S***	105
Epistle to John Rankin	113
Lament for James, Earl of Glencairn	117
Tam O' Shanter	120
On the late Captain Grose's Peregrinations thro' Scotland	130
Verses Written under the Portrait of Fergusson the Poet	133
Verses on the Destruction of the Woods near Drumlanrig	133

CONTENTS.

POEMS—*continued.*   PAGE

   The Solemn League and Covenant 136
   There's naethin like the Honest Nappy 136

SONGS :—

   My ain kind Dearie O 139
   Auld Bob Morris 140
   My Wife's a Winsome Wee Thing 141
   Duncan Gray cam' here to woo 142
   Braw Lads on Yarrow Braes 144
   Wandering Willie 145
   Logan Braes 146
   O Lassie, art thou Sleeping yet? 148
   Her Answer—O tell na me o' wind and rain 149
   Groves o' Sweet Myrtle 150
   Last May a Braw Wooer cam' down the Lang Glen. . . 151
   Blythe was she 153
   I Love my Jean 154
   Willie Brew'd a Peck o' Maut 155
   John Anderson my Jo 156
   Guidwife Count the Lawin 157
   What can a Young Lassie do wi' an Auld Man 158
   O, for Ane and Twenty, Tam ! 159
   Bess and her Spinning Wheel 160
   The Banks o' Doon 162
   Version printed in the Musical Museum 163
   For the sake o' Somebody 164
   O May, thy Morn 165
   The Lovely Lass of Inverness 166
   A red, red Rose 167
   Address to a Lady 168
   Up in the Morning Early 169
   My Bonie Mary 170

CONTENTS.   ix

Songs—*continued.*   PAGE
My Heart's in the Highlands 171
There's a Youth in this City 172
Ae Fond Kiss 173
Out over the Forth 174
John Barleycorn 175
The Rigs o' Barley 178
Song—Behind yon hills where Stinchar flows 180
Green Grow the Rashes 182
Ye Banks, and Braes, and Streams around 184
Auld Lang Syne 185
Bruce's Address to his Army at Bannockburn 187
For a' that and a' that 188
The Dumfries Volunteers 190
Mary Morison 192
O Saw ye Bonie Lesley 193
Women's Minds 194
To Mary in Heaven 196
Patriotic Song 197
Awa Whigs, Awa 199
Braw Lads of Galla Water 200
Coming through the Rye 201
Hey, the Dusty Miller 202
The Cardin' o't 203
It was a' for our Rightfu' King 204
O Kenmure's on and awa, Willie 205
Simmer's a pleasant Time 207
The Highland Laddie 208
Weary fa' you, Duncan Gray 209
Ye Jacobites by name 210
Whan I sleep I dream 211
When I think on the Happy Days 212

INTRODUCTION.

BURNS, the poetry of Burns, the life of Burns, are topics which eternally attract the critic. On few literary subjects has more been said, on none, perhaps, is it more difficult to say anything satisfactory. To say anything which shall satisfy all readers is quite out of the question. To English students, Robert Burns is, and must be, a foreign classic. People who decline to read the Waverley novels, because they "detest dialect," must find the author of "Tam o' Shanter" impossible. With the best will in the world it is tedious to look up glossaries a dozen times on each page, or to desert the text for the footnotes, twice or thrice in a line. Even when the conscientious English reader does take this trouble, he finds that a Scotch phrase may mean "excitedly eager" in one passage, and "eagerly fond" in another, while the full force, and it has a great deal, of "fidgin' fain" is only apparent to a Scot. In truth, the Scotch dialogue in the Waverley novels is classical Scotch, the Scotch of Edinburgh and the Border, while Burns delights in provincial Scotch, in Ayrshire words of which even the Scotch sometimes need an explanation. What is "muslin kail?" what is a "shangar?" what is a "stimpart?" One has put these questions to very loyal and unanglicized Scots, and they have been unable to answer. We learn little when we are told that a certain mare was a "noble fittielan'," and though "tarrow" rhymes to "Pizarro," the word is so obscure that it escaped even the older minstrel who was so hard set for various rhymes to "Yarrow." A little pains, a little acuteness, and the use of a Scottish dictionary, clear up these difficulties, but many persons are so indolent that they will rather take Burns for granted than busy themselves to understand him. It is extremely probable that, even in Scotland, Burns is more praised than read. In some places the enthusiasm of his Birthday suppers would be chilled if anyone brought in a copy of the poems and asked for a few explanations. The old language is dying out, thanks to newspapers and education, and Burns's language was extraordinarily rich in local and technical terms, which make his poems even to an Eastern or Border Scot anything but plain sailing.

The very wealth of his vocabulary, which often added brilliance to his humour, is beginning to

INTRODUCTION. xiii

turn against him. His vogue, the national enthusiasm for him, is perhaps greater than ever, but the time may come when that will be said of Burns which Voltaire said of Dante, "he will always be praised, because he is never read." However, the remark is no longer true of Dante, and a millennium or two must pass before it is true of the Ayrshire ploughman. Still, these mere initial difficulties, trivial in themselves, make it hard to write of Burns so as to satisfy most English readers. To take an obvious example: Cæsar, in "The Twa Dogs," talking of the amusements of the rich laird, says that he—

"To Madrid takes the rout,
To thrum guitars, and fecht wi' nowt."

There is no note to the word *nowt* in Mr. Scott Douglas's excellent edition. Probably the ordinary English reader does not even know that *nowt* are horned cattle in general. He certainly cannot feel the Scot's delight in this amusingly depreciatory phrase for the heroic pastime of Bull-fighting. One must have been born to the language, to understand its delicacies. This is all the harder on Burns as his Scotch poems are, by universal consent, as well as in his own opinion, infinitely his best poems. English prose he *could* write excellently, but his model, in English verse, was the divine Shenstone, whereas in Scotch verse he had Scotch tradition to guide him, and was using his everyday speech.

Thus a Scotchman, writing of Burns, will inevitably feel an enthusiasm which may seem overstrained to the general run of English readers. The language which detains and at times defies the Englishman is like his native air to the Scot, in spite of the obsolete and provincial words. It smells of peat and bog myrtle, of heather, haggis and whiskey. Burns was not invariably sincere, he answered too well to Montaigne's description of man as *ondoyant et divers*, or, if he was invariably sincere, his moods changed so frequently and so rapidly as to give an appearance of insincerity. But on one point his ideas never altered, his ardent love of his land. In some notes from his commonplace book (1784?), he mentions that it hurts him to see other regions famous in song, "their rivers, haughs, and woods immortalized," and expresses his desire to make Irvine, Ayr, and Doon "emulate Tay, Forth, Ettrick, and Tweed." "Abana and Pharpar, rivers of Syria," were, in his eyes, as good as any rivers of Israel. By their banks he listened, as he says, to "The feathered warblers," by their banks he mused, or made love: he had a poet's and an angler's love of running water, and to celebrate his native streams was literally one of his chief poetic impulses. As for the country of Scotland in general, "the story of Wallace poured a Scottish prejudice into my veins, which will boil along there till the floodgate of life shuts in eternal rest." His aim was to do something "for puir auld Scotland's sake," and it would be less than loyal if Scotchmen did not regard him with the heartiest affection and admiration. Homer was not more truly "The Sun of Hellas," as a writer in the Anthology calls him, than Burns was the Sun of Scotland. The whole life of the people, labour, religion, revelry, traditional customs, he illuminated it all, he showed it in its native colours to the world, and he warms it still. The life of the people, we say especially, for of the life of the nobles he knew little, and in spite of considerable goodwill shown by them, he loved it less. That life, so full in olden days of passion and romance, was left to the genius of Scott, a genius, to my mind, really more human, kindly, and universal, if less intense. Burns's eager love of Independence — "I am independent," he says proudly, when dedicating his poems to the gentlemen of the Caledonian Hunt,—was mainly attracted by one aspect of old Scotch history, the War of Independence, the struggle of Wallace and Bruce against the greatest and the weakest of the Plantagenets. It is evident that Burns was under a

b

delusion said, by our unfriends, to be common in Scotland. He thought that, at Bannockburn, Bruce defeated The Hammer of the Scots. In his letter to Lord Buchan, enclosing "Scots wha hae," he says, "a cruel but able usurper was leading on the finest army in Europe." These words can only apply to Edward I., *Malleus Scotorum*; the English king at Bannockburn was neither conspicuously cruel nor conspicuously able, and Aylmer de Valence may well have sighed for one hour of the First Edward.

On the theme of Bruce's wanderings Burns intended to write a drama, a piece displaying not only royal adventures, but the humours of the people. The rest of Scotch history, so dear to Sir Walter, and so nobly illustrated by him in all its aspects of passion and romance, was apparently all but ndifferent to Burns. Ruined castle, ancient *château*, fairy knoll, kelpie-haunted loch, do not occupy his Muse: he is only concerned with the grotesque and humorous traits in witchcraft, as in "Tam o' Shanter," or in the domestic magic of "Halloween." He who was so learned in Scotch songs cared comparatively little for Scotch ballads. "The old ballad, 'I wish I were where Helen lies,'" he says, "is silly to contemptibility." This is the beautiul ballad of "Helen of Kirkconnell Lee." Yet he

INTRODUCTION. xvii

had once begun a ballad collection, of which a few fragments remain. It is difficult to say why the romance and passion of the ballads moved him so little, why he left them to be collected by Scott. His patriotism, in brief, was not nearly so universal as Sir Walter's.

Thus Burns revived Scotland, if Scott did far more than Burns to bring all Scotland, and all its past, into the light of history and of general knowledge. Burns was a child of the people, of them only he cared much to sing, as a rule, and when he touched on history, he favoured one of the two periods in which the Scotch take a living interest. These are the War of Independence and the struggles of the Covenanters. In both cases the Scotch were struggling to have their own way, and they succeeded in getting it. The Covenanters, for obvious reasons, were seldom hymned by Burns; it is "Scots wha hae" that made him and keeps him the idol of his race. Now about the Covenanters, Scott was rather critical than absolutely sympathetic: he no less than Burns, appreciated the merits of Bonnie Dundee. On Wallace, he wrote no novel and no poems; on Bruce, only the comparatively unsuccessful "Lord of the Isles." Therefore, though Malachi Malagrowther was a sturdy scion of the thistle which

Burns spared in his weeding, though in the games of Sir Walter's childhood—

> "Still the Scottish lion onward bore,
> And still the English leopards fled before"—

yet, Sir Walter has never been Burns's rival in popular esteem. He was as frank and genial in private life, he "spoke to every man as if he were his blood relation," he dined and drank with all the yeomen of the Border, but "even when he was fou, he was aye the gentleman." He could not but be of gentle blood, and well aware of it; so Scott has never equalled, never will equal Burns in the general esteem of Scotchmen. We are a people of one idol, and even Mr. Gladstone will never convince his Glasgow correspondent that "the grandeur and power" of Scott's genius "raise him to such an elevation as to leave no room for an adverse claim."

While the Scotch, then, worship Burns as without an assessor on the throne of their national poetry, it is not very easy for a Scot who does not go so far, who is jealous for the other great Scottish poet, to satisfy his brethren. This little nation, so rich in minor warblers, in charming songs and ballads, has but a pair of great poets, and, to my own mind, makes too little of one, if not in certain ways too much of the other. We cannot think

INTRODUCTION.

too highly of Burns—a lyrist unapproached for some great qualities, for passion, for pathos, for energy, for simplicity, and as a humourist and Fescennine satirist also without a peer in his own domain. We cannot praise him too much, but, as Mr. Arnold said about Homer, we can praise him "too like barbarians." If I may employ a Scotch expression, we may "blether" too much about him. There used to be an old debauched hanger-on at one of Burns's haunts, who was wont to introduce himself thus to pious pilgrims, "I'm him that Robbie Burns ca'd a blethering bitch." Many orators, many after-dinner speakers, many writers of letters to the newspapers, resemble this unabashed person. They thrust Burns down our throats, in season and out of season. He is no provincial poet, but they are provincial in an admiration which, one suspects, is sometimes affected, and based more on tradition than on a knowledge of the poet's works. These Scots we cannot hope to satisfy; it is enough if we prevent them from making us dissatisfied with Burns. About that divinity, too, as of old about theology, we are a people each with a rigid orthodoxy of our own. We are as exclusive and tenacious as David Deans in our belief that we, and we alone, are without right-hand backslidings and left-hand fallings-off in our devotion to the poet. No critic can hope to satisfy so many sects, all orthodox. For example, there was Mr. Scott Douglas, a recent and most industrious editor of Burns. He was dissatisfied with M. Taine. It is a truth, though not an important truth, about the poet, that he occasionally followed bad and affected models in his English composition. M. Taine ventured to say so; to say that Burns "laboured to attain a great epistolary style . . . . he wrote to his lady-loves with choice phrases, full of periods as pedantic as Dr. Johnson's." Then M. Taine quotes :—

"O Clarinda, shall we not meet in a state— some yet unknown state of being, where the lavish hand of Plenty shall minister to the highest wish of Benevolence, and where the chill north-wind of Prudence shall never blow over the flowery field of Enjoyment." This is the passage about which Mr. Stevenson remarks, that the sentiments may be those of an Old Hawk (to which Burns compared himself), but the style is the style of a Bird of Paradise. Yet Mr. Scott Douglas was angry with that "very volatile Frenchman," M. Taine, who certainly had a perfect right to criticise the language of the letters to Clarinda.

Even the Scotch are much divided in their opinions about the character and influence of

Burns. His character, his career, are themes from which one is tempted to shrink in terror, so perilous are they. Once I ventured to say— Principal Shairp had said it before—that I wished we knew no more of Burns's life than of Shakespeare's. It was a vain thing to wish; we cannot keep his poetry, with its frequent confessions, and be ignorant of his life. But I meant no more than a natural desire to be spared sermons, scandal, tattle about a poet. I care no more to grope after the last gossip about Jean Armour, than to listen to the last "chatter about Harriet." But a critic in "Blackwood's Magazine" assailed me at once. He alleged that I attacked Burns's moral character because I wrote Scotch verses, and knew in my heart that they were not as good as Burns's, and therefore tried to blacken his reputation, as I could not be equalled with him in renown. Having written but two *ballades* in the Lowland dialect, I can honestly say that these motives of envy and jealousy had escaped my own observation. Mr. Robert Louis Stevenson, who has spoken his mind with perfect candour about Burns's life, was handed over to the tormentors in the same sentence as myself. After this amusing example, who can deny that to write about Ranting Roving Robin is a delicate and dangerous affair!

It seems to me that Burns's "moral character" was not very complicated, nor difficult to understand. The son of a peasant, upright, strict, according to some accounts irascible, Burns was born with passions of extraordinary force into a land as Puritan in principle as the ideal Israel of the Prophets, and as lax in practice as the ideal Florence of Boccaccio. The stool of repentance and the midnight tryst among the rigs of barley were complementary institutions. Burns sometimes found himself occupying the former, sometimes dallying amidst the latter. We see him now "praying under the pressure of violent anguish," now "Amang the rigs wi' Annie." There was nothing extraordinary or perplexing in this conduct. Man was made to enjoy and to repent. The only extraordinary thing was the unmatched energy of Burns in these exercises, and in his expression of emotions which he shared with the other swains and nymphs of Mauchline or of Lochlea. Sometimes Scotch principle was uppermost in his mind, sometimes Scotch practice. The Cotter's Saturday Night was now passed in devotion, now in revelry. Mr. Shairp has wondered that he who wrote "The Cotter's Saturday Night" should also have written "Holy Willy's Prayer" and "The Jolly Beggars." This is

INTRODUCTION. xxiii

merely to marvel at the nature of men, especially of poets. As a matter of historical fact, the manners of rural Scotland were no more strict in some ways than the manners of classic Sicily. The religion, the stern Puritanism, was merely a reaction, a violent reaction, in the opposite direction. Discourses from the big Ha' Bible would influence Burns when his pleasure was past; the lessons of the dancing school, the harvest field, the opportunities of Halloween would be with him at other hours. His beauty, the glow of eyes such as Scott "never saw in any other head," his wonderful magic in conversation, which, as the Duchess of Gordon said, "carried her off her feet," his fame as a poet, his power of conferring immortality, gave Burns in his world the same chances as Byron enjoyed in his own. The results were naturally not dissimilar, though Burns's heart was, apparently, far kinder and gentler and more loyal than Byron's; therefore was his career on the whole less tragical. All was lost but honour, and even the white shield of honour was not all unstained. Till he was twenty-three, Burns says, "*Vive l'amour et vive la bagatelle* were my sole principles of action." We need not describe him more harshly than he described himself. His heart, in the amatory sense, was the merest tinder, any pair of eyes were bright enough to set it in a flame. In 1787 he was twenty-eight, and went on a tour in the Border, of which he made a few notes. They are as full of *amourettes* as the diary of Mr. Samuel Pepys. Every day he meets and describes a pretty girl, sometimes three or four of them. "May 10. *Nota bene*, the Poet within a point and a half of being damnably in love." There is a *bruit* about him and a Miss Lindsay. He presents her with "a proof print of my Nob, which she accepted with something more tender than gratitude." Next day, Lady Don is "a divine lady." Three days later, "my Bardship's heart got a brush from Miss Betsey Grieve." Immediately after he calls on "Heavenly powers, who know the weakness of human hearts," to support *his* against Miss Ainslie. At Carlisle he makes a tryst with yet another young woman, and gives her a bottle of cider: "she sheers off." All this time he was entangled with, and though he did not know it, seems to have been married to Miss Armour. His heart, too, had been recently broken by the death of his Highland Mary, to whom he had been solemnly betrothed. What is there to be said of so general and wayward a lover? We can only say that, in these affairs, his character and conduct were perfectly consistent, now with his passions, now with his principles. Most of us may throw the first stone at so egregious a sinner, may set the collies after so incorrigibly wandering a sheep. But most of us have scarcely an idea of Burns's opportunities and temptations, which were quite as rare as his conduct. It is equally easy, and, to different natures, equally tempting, to applaud this genius, or to condemn him : another thing should not be more difficult, namely, to understand him.

His relations with women, no doubt, are complex enough. Though his heart was tinder, it was not cruel; it got the better of his Don Juanism, and he married Jean Armour. No one, probably, had suffered more than she for his sake, and he made up his mind to endure matrimony, and to make the best of it, for hers. It is rather a dismal business, making the best of it. His wife, he says, is a "clean-limbed, handsome, bewitching young hussey."

"Bode a robe and wear it,
Bode a poke, and bear it."

He bore the poke as well as he might. "I can easily fancy a more agreeable partner for my journey of life ; but, upon my honour, I have never seen the individual instance." Jean had "a native wood note wild," and "a sacred enthusiasm of affection" for him. He argued that he never could have won an educated woman, who would have "relished his favourite authors," yet would not have plagued him with "blessed boarding-school acquirements." "The females of the upper ranks" were out of his reach, "the misses of the would-be gentry" were not to his mind. Had he been free, and had she been free, he might have married Clarinda, who did not find his behaviour satisfactory. But—

"His honour rooted in dishonour stood,
And faith unfaithful kept him falsely true."

His life, he told Clarinda, "damns me with a choice only of different species of error and misconduct."

He felt that he had partly frittered away the power of knowing what married love is, the love of which Odysseus says that—

"There is nothing nobler nor more of might."

It is not easy for us to say, he could scarcely have said himself, what he felt for Clarinda, what he had felt for Highland Mary. Certainly what he felt for both was not what Jean Armour would have liked him to feel. To him, as perhaps to all but the best and happiest, the Ideal had always to be the Unattained. Meanwhile, in the economy of the universe, so strangely contrary to our moralities, the end of all his amours was a charm of beautiful songs. Heroes died in war of old, "that there might be a song in the ears of men to come." Women have died in love, too, or have lived in sorrow to this same result, that there might be a song in the ears of folk unborn. For a song Burns sold his life; all ends in song. This alone lives! The poet is dead, and dead are the fair ladies and the pretty wenches—Miss Lindsay, Miss Ainslie, Miss Grieve, and the girl who drank the bottle of cider, and many another lass, named or unnamed in the chronicle of his heart. The cider is drunk out, the lips that kissed, the hearts that broke, are dust; only the songs survive:

"Still are thy pleasant voices, thy nightingales awake,
For Death takes everything away, but these he cannot take."

It is not for us to condemn Burns, nor to absolve his arts as "seeming genial venial faults." He who wrote—

"Is there in human form that bears a heart,
  A wretch! a villain! lost to love and truth!
That can with studied, sly, unsparing art
  Betray sweet Jenny's unsuspecting youth?
Curse on his perjured arts, dissembling smooth!
  Are human virtue, conscience, all exiled

> Is there no pity, no relenting ruth,
> Points to the parents fondling o'er their child?
> Then paints the ruined maid, and their distraction wild"—

was a man eminent for his intrigues. Mr. Armour's "distraction wild" was proved by his fainting when he heard of the "ruin" of his daughter Jean. The "old hawk," as Burns called himself, was also the denouncer of "studied, sly, unsparing art." He was running after Jean exactly at the time when he was writing about the "Cotter's Saturday Night," its rural virtues and pious exercises. Not by us, but by Burns himself, is he to be judged, and the nature of things condemned him. About all light love he says—

> "But oh! it hardens a' within
> And petrifies the feeling."

Fortunately against his form of a poet's love we can set the immortal passion of Scott, his heart which was two years broken, and then "handsomely mended," but which, thirty years after all was done, could still be stirred by the memory of the name that he had once carved, in Runic letters, on the turf by the ruined castle-gate in St. Andrews. The heart of Burns, after Highland Mary's death, was, as we have seen, much more rapidly repaired. But, to Scott, his one love was too sacred to be versified upon. In his longer poems and his novels alone that memory moves enchanted and disguised. In "To Mary in Heaven," Burns, after a sleepless night on the banks of the Nith, gave voice to what we may presume to have been his purest and most unalterable affection. Mary's memory, at least is "like a star,"—" the lingering star with lessening ray that loves to greet the early morn "—and " dwells apart."

The other feature in Burns's character concerning which there has been dispute and moralizing, is, of course, his attachment to Scottish drink. Little need be said about it. The age was devoted to hard drinking. Burns often complains of the local whiskey, the execrable whiskey of Dumfriesshire. He complains of "the savage hospitality" that knocks a man down with ardent liquors. He satirizes the orgies in his own house after the sale of his year's harvest. Probably he was far from being an intemperate man in the judgment of his age, till many disappointments, failures, sorrows, wore him down. "Even in the hour of social mirth," he writes to Aiken as early as 1786, " my gaiety is the madness of an intoxicated criminal under the hands of the executioner." He wrote Bacchanalian ditties many, as he wrote other ditties, in "The Merry Muses." These were concessions to the taste of his companions. In his last years, perhaps, he may have sought to forget his many miseries in an artificial Paradise. His mistake was the common mistake of his period and country: nothing would have been heard of it had he not been great.

The indulgence of these passions, or their absence, or the mastery of them, is not the whole of morality. Burns had in the highest measure the masculine virtues. He was kind; there was nothing he hated like unkindness. Lockhart mentions an old Galloway laird and magistrate who was indifferent to poetry, but loved the goodness of heart which Burns showed in his official reports as an exciseman. He was honest, and upright, and generous. If he had been "rich as the sun," he says, he would have been "generous as the day." He lent his brother Gilbert a large proportion of the four or five hundred pounds he made by his poems. For his songs in Thomson's collection he absolutely refused to take money. In song, like that Theocritean Cyclops, he "found more happiness than could be bought by gold," and he would not allow gold to be brought into the sacred place of the Muses. We may regret the scruple, but we must respect it. He honestly

INTRODUCTION. xxxi

laboured to support his family by the work of his hands. Farming was not successful with him, partly for want of capital perhaps, partly because he reasoned, "if miry ridges and dirty dunghills are to engross the better functions of a soul immortal, I had better have been a rook or magpie at once." When he took the resolution to become an exciseman, he may not have calculated prudently, but he displayed a noble courage in disregarding cheap satire and the paper bullets of the brain. The idea of gaining some secure income for his family,

> "To make a happy fireside clime
> For weans and wife,"

by duties in no way dishonourable, mastered all fear of dependence and all dread of ridicule.

What should Burns have done? what should have been done for Burns? These are questions often asked, but in practice not to be answered. Probably he would not have allowed anyone to give him a farm free of rent, as the Duke of Buccleuch did to James Hogg. In the copious patronage of the time we cannot but think that a higher office than that of a gauger might have been found for him, had he chanced to be on the dominant side in politics. No such post was found. The profession of literature, as we understand it now, as even Hogg found it not unremunerative, scarcely existed, at least in Scotland. Burns could not have been a journalist, or an editor; probably he never dreamed of being a novelist, or of living by the theatre. To succeed in any of those fields he must have dwelt in England, which he would have 'found impossible. Burns in London is inconceivable, though London, if he could have endured it, might have proved less fatal to him than Dumfries.

The religion of Burns was rather a religion of hope than of belief. Brought up among peasant Puritans, and ardently admiring what was beautiful in the old Scotch faith, Burns early made the acquaintance of "The Moderates," the refined, philosophical, and more or less easy-going ministers of his day. The Moderates are often accused of having injured his character by critics who perhaps know very little about their writings and nothing but some traditional stories about their lives. Burns was unfortunate enough to see the Holy Willies of his district, to behold the orgies of their revival meetings and holy fairs. As nothing was more sternly solemn than the one annual sacrament of the Scottish Church, so nothing can have been more deserving of satire

INTRODUCTION. xxxiii

than the corruptions which Burns describes, if he describes them truly. That was probably what his victims denied. For all we know, Mr. Moodie, who "cleared the points o' faith," may have been as excellent a man as Smith of the "cauld harangues." But Burns was on the other side. The clergy of the Auld Lichts, the evangelical clergy, had subjected him to ecclesiastical censure—a discipline perhaps always inefficient outside of the Church of Rome, and by Burns's time half obsolete and wholly ludicrous. For himself, as he told Mrs. Dunlop, religion was "his dearest enjoyment . . . . an irreligious poet is a monster." He was usually prepared to admit his belief in God and immortality, to grant that Jesus Christ was "from God."

> "A Power from the Unknown God,
> A Promethean conqueror came."

As for immortality, in a moment of depression he cries, "Would to God that I as firmly believed it as I ardently wish it!" In a more flippant humour he observes, "If there be any truth in the orthodox faith of these churches, I am damned past redemption" (which surely is not "the orthodox faith of these churches") . . . . so I shall e'en turn Arminian, and trust to 'sincere though imperfect obedience.'" He had widened the already wide and more or less Arminian creed of his excellent father. He believed that religion was necessary for goodness and for happiness, and he instructed his children and the boys about his farm in its doctrines. In brief, he had as much religion as was possible to a man of his genius, passions, and circumstances, in the intellectual tempest of his age.

In religion, as in politics, Burns is well fitted by the motto chosen for him from George Buchanan by his recent editor, Mr. Scott Douglas :—

"Salve, vetustæ vitæ imago
Et specimen venientis Ævi."

Much of the old Covenanting Scotland, much of the old Scotland of song, of love, of revel, was in him, much also of Democracy, both in its pride of independent labour and in its unfriendliness to the rich and well-born. "He had always," says his brother Gilbert, "a particular jealousy of people who were richer than himself, or who had more consequence in life." He rails, in a fragment of a diary, against persons who drive in carriages, and splash the Edinburgh mud on him, Robert Burns. They were born to wealth, he was born to genius ; really the one accident is not more unfair

INTRODUCTION. xxxv

than the other. But he thought the chance of birth unfair; he thought that his merit was neglected, being perfectly, though far from inordinately, conscious of his merit. Yet it may be said that Burns received infinitely more kindness from dukes and earls, Glencairns, Athols, and Gordons (as did James Hogg too), from the proud and secure *noblesse* of his day, than genius like his would now obtain from the very insecure *noblesse* of our age.

It is universally acknowledged that among the great, and even among the learned and critical, Burns bore himself with perfect ease and equanimity. Probably it was his relations with the local gentry, which began in jollity and ended in strife, that made him so detest their order. In later years, as in the case of Mrs. Riddell, he behaved ill, recanted, behaved worse, and made himself for a time impossible as a guest and intimate. The extreme toils of his laborious boyhood, the spectacle of a factor's cruel insolence, and of his father's poverty and sorrow, were much more legitimate causes than any minor social troubles, of his bitterness. Who would not have been embittered? It may be that the doing of a man's work when he was a boy of fifteen injured the health of Burns quite as much as did the excesses of his later life. Certainly his democratic mood, his conviction that "a man's a man for a' that," has endeared him as much as any other quality of his, as much as his music, pathos, romance, to the Scotch people. He is their champion, their spokesman, their ideal. It is said to be inconsistent with his democratic ideas that he was not out of sympathy with Jacobitism, any more than he was out of sympathy with the French Revolution. In truth he was no partisan. "I am not man enough to have any political attachments," he writes, and remarks that he has friends in both parties. He was a poet, and so forlorn causes were dear to him. As to the Stuarts, he saw, and said, that in their time a struggle between prince and people was inevitable. "The Stuarts only contended for prerogatives which they knew their predecessors enjoyed, and which they saw their contemporaries enjoying." This is to speak not only in a sober historical spirit, but, as Professor Blackie might say, "like a gentleman." "Let every man who has a tear for the many miseries incident to humanity feel for a family illustrious as any in Europe, and unfortunate beyond historic precedent; and let every Briton (and particularly every Scotsman) who ever looked on the dotage of a parent cast a veil over the fatal mistakes of the kings of his forefathers." In this letter to the editor of the "Star," Burns is no Jacobite; even his touching and stirring Jacobite songs are not political, unless Macaulay is stamped a Jacobite by the most tender and melancholy of his poems.

The Muses are maidens, and therefore they lament the dear ruined cause, as they wailed over the pyre of Achilles.

"Victrix causa deis placuit, sed victa puellis."

As to his partisanship of the French Revolution, Burns was probably sooner disgusted with that orgie than Wordsworth. In 1792, in a letter to Mrs. Dunlop, he speaks of France as "convulsed with every horror that can harrow the human feelings," and when we were threatened with war he wrote the most stirring patriotic songs. In truth, he was not too little, but too much of a man to be a party politician. He was on the side of the unhappy, whether they were kings or cotters. To be short, as a man he was passionate indeed, reckless at times, repentant often, a victim of revel and remorse, but he was also kindly, brave, witty, brilliant, upright, generous, pitiful; and as a friend so tolerant and loyal, that he endured without a sign of ill-temper the jealous envy of the detestable William Nichol, though, in later years, he could not accept the reproofs of that sot and bully.

In the poetry of Burns, the chief impulses are love, music, patriotism, satire, pity, and enjoyment of nature. His earliest piece, written at about the age of fifteen, begins, " O once I lov'd a bonnie lass," a bonnie lass among whose charming qualities he mentions that "she sang sweetly . . . and it was her favourite reel to which I attempted giving an embodied vehicle in rhyme." As he began, so he went on, and so he ended. The poetic work of his later years was almost entirely song-writing. He was kindled by the eyes of Chloris, or by the golden locks of Anna; he then mused on an old Scotch tune, perhaps he borrowed a line or a verse of an old Scotch song, and so he beat his music out. His were true lyrics; they all came singing to him, they were all meant to be sung rather than to be read. Before Burns's day Allan Ramsay had greatly tampered with the words of ancient Scotch popular lyrics—tampered with them and substituted his own phrases so much that these songs of old centuries have almost perished. Enough remain to show that the words were often silly and often coarse, yet their disappearance is a thing to be bitterly regretted by students of popular literature. It is a mere truism to say that Burns purified his national ditties, and gave us golden words for words of very doubtful metal. Still, the spirit of the antiquarian hankers after even "the veniable part of things lost," in spite of the splendid substitute. It were superfluous to praise the songs of Burns, the verses with which he began and concluded his poetical career. They fly about the world on the wings of music, and are chanted wherever Scotchmen meet, that is, wherever man can live. Everyone has his own peculiar favourites: the delicate pathos of "Mary Morison," like the natural speech of a heart which is tender and true; the more reckless rapture of "The Rigs o' Barley;" the glad and sportive autumnal cadence of "Now westlin' winds and slaught'ring guns;" the domestic charm of "My Nannie, O." This is a delightful picture of Theocritean wooing, with the contrast between the dark outward night,—

"where Stinchar flows,
'Mang moors and mosses many, O"—

and the warm cottage fireside where the singer goes to meet his love. Mr. Matthew Arnold has remarked that "Burns's world of Scotch drink, Scotch religion, and Scotch manners is often a hard, a sordid, a repulsive world." Yet we may compare this winter love-scene in Ayrshire with another in Sicily, and not find the contrast too extreme.

It is true enough that "this world of Scotch drink, Scotch religion, and Scotch manners is against a poet." We are certainly *not* "in Sicily to-day," the religion, the climate, the *vin du pays* are very different, but as to the *manners*, the contrast is rather in favour of the Northern people. At all events, limited as Burns undoubtedly is by his Caledonian circumstances, he has versatility and variety enough. Song can scarcely be gayer than in "Green grow the Rashes, O," nor "pawkier" than in "Indeed will I, quo' Findlay." "Macpherson's Farewell," in an utterly different strain, is worthy of the bold outlaw; above all, if Burns, and not tradition, produced the chorus:—

"Sae rantingly, sae wantonly,
Sae dauntingly gaed he;
He played a spring and danced it round,
Below the gallow's tree."

Then there is the charming set of songs written to Mrs. Burns after Burns had married her. It really seemed as if he could make the best of it, when he composed for his own wedded wife (a character rarely the subject of a poet's song),—

"O' a' the airts the winds can blaw,
I dearly like the west."

INTRODUCTION. xli

Tradition gave him the lines which have been compared for direct and intense energy to the lyrics of Catullus,—

> "Go, fetch to me a pint o' wine,
> And fill it in a silver tassie"—

but Burns, in his continuation of the piece, scarcely fell below his model. "The Banks o' Doon," in any of its variants, is a little masterpiece, though we may prefer the second version to the trailing redundancies which music was supposed to demand in the third. The "Parting Song to Clarinda" contains perhaps the most passionate verse even in Burns's poetry, "the essence of a thousand love-tales," said Scott :—

> "Had we never loved sae kindly,
> Had we never loved sae blindly,
> Never met or never parted,
> We had ne'er been broken-hearted."

There is a gallant and chivalrous accent in—

> "O saw ye bonnie Leslie,
> As she gaed o'er the Border?"

and while Scotland stands, Scotch sentiment will never forget—

> "Ye banks and braes and streams around
> The Castle o' Montgomery;"

a piece so much akin to the antique manner that it relies on assonance, not on rhyme. Probably to

Burns, not to tradition, we owe the lines so highly praised by Mr. Carlyle :—

> "The wan moon is setting behind the white wave,
>   And Time is setting with me, O,"

though about the real authorship there is no certainty. The famous "Scots wha hae" has certainly not wanted its meed of applause; perhaps it is difficult quite to estimate words so excessively familiar to the ear of every Scot. Burns's misapprehension about Edward I. has already been remarked on. It does not seem absolutely certain that Burns wrote the words which Scott repeated among the ruins of Italy,—

> "It's up yon heathery mountain,
>   An' down yon rocky glen,
>   We daur na gang a-milking
>   For Charlie and his men."

But Mr. Scott Douglas has made out an almost perfect plea for Burns's authorship of that most beautiful Jacobite lay,—

> "It was a' for our rightfu' king,
>   We left fair Scotland's strand."

It was a great favourite of Sir Walter's, who liked to hear it sung from the pages of Johnson, to whom Burns sent it. The gallant lines which Sir Walter introduced into "Rokeby,"—

> "He turned him right and round about,
>   Upon the Irish shore,"

occur in a stall-ballad, clearly an interpolation there. Sir Walter thought they were old; Mr. Scott Douglas "has no doubt that the broadside referred to was printed after 1796." But the grounds of his confidence are not given, and I myself venture to agree with Sir Walter. It is a matter of conjecture, but to me the verse does not read like Burns's work.

These are but gems, noted for one dominant quality or another, in the great treasure of Burns's lyrics. There are also plenty of frivolous and unimportant songs, hastily turned out to fit the tune, but these do not diminish the pathos of "John Anderson," nor the quiet fun of "Duncan Gray cam' here to woo," nor the rather fatuous gaiety of "Ye Mauchline Belles." Perhaps, in the world, and in the poetry of all peoples, there is nothing, unless it be the somewhat analogous poetry of Béranger, to match with the songs of Burns. Both are absolutely of the people and for the people, both show a patriotism which some may deem exuberant. But even an exuberant patriotism is better than a rooted belief that love of native land, and pride in it, are identical with the worship of the great god Jingo. It is of little service to compare Burns to Horace; two lyrists could hardly be more dissimilar. Burns has passion; Horace had, or displayed none. Horace followed Greek models; Burns went in the path of the old Scotch Casmenæ. Horace was a courtier, and the most gracefully artificial of artists; Burns was preeminently a rustic, and his art was of the sort that conceals itself, being utterly spontaneous, simple, direct, though not disdainful of labour, and guided by a natural excellence of taste. Among classical authors, Burns resembles Catullus in amorous passion, in shame, repentance, in satiric indignation, in love of home and the beautiful country where he was born. His rural pictures, "Tam o' Shanter" and "Halloween," may be compared to the best idylls of Theocritus in everything but that perfect beauty only attainable by a Greek, only possible in the light and air of classical landscape. Burns probably knew Theocritus, or divined him, as he knew Homer and Virgil, through translations. But it was not to the Syracusan example that he owed his habit of drawing rural life as it really was; his exemplars, as he always acknowledged, were Fergusson and Allan Ramsay. His generous devotion to the memory and fair renown of the short-lived and unfortunate Fergusson is always breaking out in his verse, as in his erection of a monument over the poet's grave. He, the master, regarded himself as the disciple, and it is no doubt true that his favourite measure was borrowed from Ramsay and Fergusson, while Fergusson's picture of a cottage home, his sketches of Edinburgh life, may have suggested to Burns his first essays in similar fields. The young St. Andrews student, who died, sane as it seems, in a madhouse, had humour, had a singular veracity in description, but of Burns's passion, of his ardour, of his intimate sense of nature, Fergusson had scarcely a trace. There are no love poems in his only valuable verses, those written in Scotch. His English imitations are beneath notice, and immeasurably beneath the least successful efforts of Burns in the Southern tongue. There was a Scotch quality which Burns did not possess. He knew his worth, but he was as devoid of conceit as of literary jealousy. Scott, who when a boy saw him once, says, "I thought his acquaintance with English poetry was rather limited, and also that, having twenty times the abilities of Allan Ramsay and of Fergusson, he talked of them with too much humility as his models. There was, doubtless, national predilection in his estimate."

They were his models, in a way; the idea of designing such pictures as "Halloween," "The Cotter's Saturday Night," and "Tam o' Shanter," the idea of a dialogue between "The Brigs o' Ayr," was derived from Fergusson. But, with all respect for the memory of Fergusson, he gave the example and the impulse, but little more. Fergusson's "Farmer's Ingle," indeed, may perhaps even be preferred, for veracity and absence of self-consciousness, to the more famous "Cotter's Saturday Night," which has eclipsed without excelling it. Fergusson was but twenty-four when he died; what he might have achieved is unknown. But he gave little promise of equalling Burns's extraordinary vigour, his wealth of invention and imagination, his kindliness, his humour, his energy of satire. It is superfluous to dwell on these merits: on the unequalled daring and prodigal genius of "The Jolly Beggars;" the wisdom and wit of the "Twa Dogs," and of the "Epistle to Davie;" on "Tam o' Shanter," the brief epic of Scotch *diablerie*; on Burns's many examples of all that one admires in Cuddie Headrigg, Edie Ochiltree, and all Scott's throng of peasant characters. Inimitable, and unimitated, are the humorous pity and kindness of the "Farmer's Good Year to his Auld Mare," and the verses on the Mouse and the Daisy. Burns is, beyond all possibility of rivalry, the greatest of all truly popular poets.

Other nations, like the Irish, have lost much, if not all of their popular poetry, through modern education, schools, the clergy, and the newspapers. Burns, appearing at the nick of time, preserved all that was best of the popular poetry except the ballads, in forms which are at once truly popular and immortal as literature. As Lockhart observes, he revived the Scottish nationality, which was falling asleep in the graves of the Stuarts. The rest was done by Scott.

I had written this, trusting rather heedlessly to Lockart's authority, when I was warned that, after all, Scotch nationality was by no means extinct in Burns's time, that the embers were still aglow. "Strange as it may now appear," writes an excellent authority, "I am inclined to think that the publication of Ossian, immediately before Burns, did more to exalt the national feeling of Scotland, and to diffuse its fame, than Burns's Poems, though Ossian has vanished like a comet, and Burns is an everlasting star." And, on reflection, this is obviously true. The pious three-quarters fraud of Macpherson did really revive, or was the occasion for a revival of Scotch national pride. Ossian carried the name and fame of Scotland abroad to France; we know that Napoleon liked "Ocean," as he spelled the word; we do not know that he ever heard of Burns. A glance at Boswell's "Life of Dr. Johnson" is enough to show how Ossian stirred Scotch pride and sentiment: how the learned Scots stood up to the Doctor in favour of Coila's bard, and the "Tour in Scotland" is full of examples both of national spirit and of national conceit. Young Fergusson, in particular, wrote an amusing poem, in which he describes the appallingly national dinner which *he* would have ordered for Dr. Johnson at St. Andrews. "There is," my critic, or rather Lockhart's critic, goes on, "as much genuine national feeling in 'Humphrey Clinker,' and in Smollett's 'Tears of Scotland,' as in Burns. And there was a more genuine love of Scotch melody and Scotch songs between the ages of Ramsay and Burns, than there has ever been since, much more than there is now." One has only to mention Mrs. Cockburn's "Flowers o' the Forest" to prove this, and Fergusson need not have cried

> "O Scotland, that could yence afford
> To bang the pith of Roman sword,
> Winna your sons, wi' joint accord
>   To battle speed?
> And fight till Music be restored
>   Which now lies dead."

Scotch music was lively enough, and, even without Burns, Thomson would have published the Scotch songs. My critic continues, "I read a beautiful anecdote somewhere, (I cannot remember the place), which I may have mentioned to you. A

Whig gentleman who had gone to Rome shortly after 1715 went to sup with some Jacobite exiles. After supper, a lady was asked to sing a Scots song; she sang "The Broom of Cowden Knowes," and when the Whig gentleman looked up and round, he saw that all the company were in tears."

No doubt Scotch sentiment was not dead, in any rank, nor dying. We must qualify Lockhart's remarks, and say that Burns did not revive it from the tomb, but merely gave it new force, especially among the people who knew not Ossian, neither regarded Smollett. But the purely popular writings of Fergusson, though they never attained the circulation which they deserved, prove that the people, too, was patriotic.

The profession of the critic is plied in constant disregard of the warning, "judge not, that ye be not judged." And, when all is said, little remains but a sense of injustice in all judgments passed on Burns. We wish him to have been this, and not that, to have been himself, and not himself. In the mystery of character and genius, in the double operation of the one flame which glows in a man's poetry, and in his personal existence, one cannot seriously pretend to divide and discern, to demand of the fire that it shall burn where it listeth here, and not there. Wordsworth says of Burns, "It is probable that he would have proved a still greater poet, if, by strength of reason, he could have controlled the propensities which his sensibilities engendered; but he would have been a poet of a different class; and certain it is, had that desirable restraint been early established, many peculiar beauties which enrich his verses could never have existed, and many necessary influences, which contribute greatly to their effect, would have been wanting." In this temperate wisdom, we really have the last word on the character and genius of Burns.

POEMS.

THE TWA DOGS.

A TALE.

'TWAS in that place o' Scotland's isle,
    That bears the name o' auld king COIL,
Upon a bonie day in June,
When wearing thro' the afternoon,
Twa dogs, that were na thrang at hame,
Forgather'd ance upon a time.
    The first I'll name, they ca'd him *Cæsar*,
Was keepit for His Honor's pleasure:
His hair, his size, his mouth, his lugs,
Shew'd he was nane o' Scotland's dogs;
But whalpet some place far abroad,
Whare sailors gang to fish for Cod.
    His locked, letter'd, braw brass collar,
Shew'd him the *gentleman and scholar;*
But tho' he was o' high degree,
The fient a pride—nae pride had he;

But wad hae spent an hour caressan,
Ev'n wi' a Tinkler-gipsey's messan.
At Kirk or Market, Mill or Smiddie,
Nae tawted tyke, tho' e'er sae duddie,
But he wad stan't, as glad to see him,
An' stroan't on stanes and hillocks wi' him.

   The tither was a *ploughman's collie*,
A rhyming, ranting, raving billie,
Wha for his friend and comrade had him,
An' in his freaks had *Luath* ca'd him,
After some dog in *Highland sang*,
Was made lang syne,—Lord knows how lang.

   He was a gash an' faithfu' *tyke*,
As ever lap a sheugh or dike.
His honest, sonsie, baws'nt face,
Ay gat him friends in ilka place;
His breast was white, his towzie back
Weel clad wi' coat o' glossy black;
His gawcie tail, wi' upward curl,
Hung owre his hurdies wi' a swirl.

   Nae doubt but they were fain o' ither,
An' unco pack an' thick thegither;
Wi' social nose whyles snuff'd and snowket;
Whyles mice and moudewurts they howket;
Whyles scour'd awa in lang excursion,
An' worry'd ither in diversion;
[Until wi' daffin weary grown,

Upon a knowe they sat them down,]
An' there began a lang digression
About the *lords o' the creation*.

CÆSAR.

I've aften wonder'd, honest *Luath*,
What sort o' life poor dogs like you have ;
An' when the *gentry's* life I saw,
What way *poor bodies* liv'd ava.
  Our *Laird* gets in his racked rents,
His coals, his kane, an' a' his stents :
He rises when he likes himsel ;
His flunkies answer at the bell ;
He ca's his coach ; he ca's his horse ;
He draws a bonie, silken purse
As lang's my tail, whare thro' the steeks,
The yellow letter'd *Geordie* keeks.
  Frae morn to e'en it's nought but toiling,
At baking, roasting, frying, boiling ;
An' tho' the gentry first are steghan,
Yet ev'n the ha' folk fill their pechan,
Wi' sauce, ragouts, and such like trashtrie,
That's little short o' downright wastrie.
Our *Whipper-in*, wee, blastit wonner,
Poor, worthless elf, it eats a dinner,
Better than ony Tenant man
His Honor has in a' the lan :

An' what poor *Cot-folk* pit their painch in,
I own it's past my comprehension.

LUATH.

Trowth, Cæsar, whyles they're fash't eneugh :
A cotter howkan in a sheugh,
Wi' dirty stanes biggin a dyke,
Baran a quarry, and sic like,
Himsel, a wife, he thus sustains,
A smytrie o' wee, duddie weans,
An' nought but his han' durk, to keep
Them right an' tight in thack an' raep.
   An' when they meet wi' sair disasters,
Like loss o' health, or want o' masters,
Ye maist wad think, a wee touch langer,
An' they maun starve o' cauld and hunger;
But, how it comes, I never kend yet,
They're maistly wonderfu' contented;
An' buirdly chiels, an' clever hizzies,
Are bred in sic a way as this is.

CÆSAR.

But then, to see how ye're neglekit,
How huff'd, an' cuff'd, an' disrespekit!
Lord, man, our gentry care as little
For delvers, ditchers, an' sic cattle,

They gang as saucy by poor folk,
As I wad by a stinkan brock.

   I've notic'd, on our Laird's *court-day*,
An' mony a time my heart's been wae,
Poor *tenant bodies*, scant o' cash,
How they maun thole a *factor's* snash ;
He'll stamp an' threaten, curse an' swear,
He'll *apprehend* them, *poind* their gear ;
While they maun stan', wi' aspect humble,
An' hear it a', an' fear an' tremble !

   I see how folk live that hae riches ;
But surely poor-folk maun be wretches.

LUATH.
   They're no sae wretched's ane wad think ;
Tho' constantly on poortith's brink,
They're sae accustom'd wi' the sight,
The view o't gies them little fright.

   Then chance an' fortune are sae guided,
They're ay in less or mair provided ;
An' tho' fatigu'd wi' close employment,
A blink o' rest's a sweet enjoyment.

   The dearest comfort o' their lives,
Their grushie weans an' faithfu' wives ;

The prattling things are just their pride,
That sweetens a' their fireside.

An' whyles twalpennie-worth o' nappy
Can mak the bodies unco happy;
They lay aside their private cares,
To mind the Kirk and State affairs;
They'll talk o' *patronage* an' *priests*,
Wi' kindling fury i' their breasts,
Or tell what new taxation's comin,
An' ferlie at the folk in LON'ON.

As bleak-fac'd Hallowmass returns,
They get the jovial, rantan kirns,
When rural life, o' ev'ry station,
Unite in common recreation;
Love blinks, Wit slaps, an' social Mirth
Forgets there's *Care* upo' the earth.

That *merry day* the year begins,
They bar the door on frosty winds;
The nappy reeks wi' mantling ream,
An' sheds a heart-inspiring steam;
The luntan pipe, an' sneeshin mill,
Are handed round wi' right guid will;
The cantie, auld folks, crackan crouse,
The young anes ranting thro' the house,—

My heart has been sae fain to see them,
That I for joy hae barket wi' them.

   Still its owre true that ye hae said,
Sic game is now owre aften play'd ;
There's monie a creditable stock
O' decent, honest, fawsont folk,
Are riven out baith root an' branch,
Some rascal's pridefu' greed to quench,
Wha thinks to knit himsel the faster
In favour wi' some *gentle Master*,
Wha aiblins thrang a parliamentin,
For Britain's guid his saul indentin—

CÆSAR.

   Haith lad ye little ken about it ;
For Britain's guid! guid faith ! I doubt it.
Say rather, gaun as PREMIERS lead him,
An' saying *aye* or *no's* they bid him :
At Operas an' Plays parading,
Mortgaging, gambling, masquerading :
Or maybe, in a frolic daft,
To HAGUE or CALAIS taks a waft,
To make a tour, an' tak a whirl,
To learn *bon ton* an' see the worl'.

   There, at Vienna or Versailles,
He rives his father's auld entails ;

Or by MADRID he taks the rout,
To thrum guittars, an' fecht wi' nowt;
Or down Italian vista startles,
Whore-hunting amang groves o' myrtles:
Then bouses drumly German-water,
To mak himsel look fair and fatter,
[An' clear the consequential sorrows,
Love gifts of carnival signoras.]
For Britain's guid! for her destruction!
Wi' dissipation, feud, an' faction!

LUATH.

Hech man! dear sirs! is that the gate
They waste sae mony a braw estate?
Are we sae foughten an' harass'd
For gear to gang that gate at last?

O would they stay aback frae courts,
An' please themsels wi' countra sports,
It wad for ev'ry ane be better,
The *Laird*, the *Tenant*, an' the *Cotter!*
For thae frank, rantan, ramblan billies,
Fient haet o' them's ill-hearted fellows;
Except for breakin o' their timmer,
Or speaking lightly o' their Limmer,
Or shootin o' a hare, or moorcock,
The ne'er-a-bit they're ill to poor folk.

But will ye tell me, Master *Cæsar*,
Sure *great folk's* life's a life o' pleasure?
Nae cauld nor hunger e'er can steer them,
The vera thought o't need na fear them.

CÆSAR.
Lord, man, were ye but whyles where I am,
The gentles ye wad neer envy 'em.

It's true, they need na starve or sweat,
Thro' Winter's cauld, or Simmer's heat;
They've nae sair-wark to craze their banes:
An' fill *auld-age* wi' grips an' granes:
But *human-bodies* are sic fools,
For a' their colledges and schools,
That when nae *real* ills perplex them,
They *mak* enow themsels to vex them;
An' ay the less they hae to sturt them,
In like proportion, less will hurt them.

A country fellow at the pleugh,
His *acre's* till'd, he's right eneugh;
A country girl at her wheel,
Her *dizzen's* done, she's unco weel:
But Gentlemen, an' Ladies warst,
Wi' ev'n down *want o' wark* are curst.
They loiter, lounging, lank, an' lazy;
Tho' deil-haet ails them, yet uneasy;

Their days insipid, dull, an' tasteless,
Their nights unquiet, lang an' restless;

An' ev'n their sports, their balls an' races,
Their galloping thro' public places,
There's sic parade, sic pomp an' art,
The joy can scarcely reach the heart.

The men cast out in party-matches,
Then sowther a' in deep debauches.
Ae night, they're mad wi' drink an' whoring,
Niest day their life is past enduring.
The *Ladies* arm-in-arm in clusters,
As great an' gracious a' as sisters;
But hear their *absent thoughts* o' ither,
They're a' run deils an' jads thegither.
Whyles, owre the wee bit cup an' platie,
They sip the scandal-potion pretty;
Or lee-lang nights, wi' crabbet leuks,
Pore ower the devil's *pictur'd beuks*;
Stake on a chance a farmer's stack-yard,
An' cheat like ony *unhang'd blackguard*.

There's some exceptions, man an' woman;
But this is Gentry's life in common.

By this, the sun was out o' sight,
An' darker gloamin brought the night:

The *bum-clock* humm'd wi' lazy drone,
The kye stood rowtin i' the loan;
When up they gat, an' shook their lugs,
Rejoic'd they were na *men* but *dogs;*
An' each took aff his several way,
Resolv'd to meet some ither day.

SCOTCH DRINK.

Gie him strong drink, until he wink,
   That's sinking in despair;
An' liquor guid to fire his bluid,
   That's prest wi' grief an' care;
There let him bouse, an' deep carouse,
   Wi' bumpers flowing o'er,
Till he forgets his loves or debts,
   An' minds his griefs no more.
               SOLOMON'S PROVERBS, xxxi. 6, 7.

LET other Poets raise a fracas
    'Bout vines, an' wines, an' druken Bacchus,
An' crabbit names an' stories wrack us,
         An' grate our lug,
I sing the juice *Scotch bear* can mak us,
         In glass or jug.

O thou, my MUSE ! guid, auld SCOTCH DRINK,
Whether thro' wimplin worms thou jink,
Or, richly brown, ream owre the brink,
    In glorious faem,
Inspire me, till I *lisp* an' *wink*,
    To sing thy name !

Let husky Wheat the haughs adorn,
An' Aits set up their awnie horn,
An' Pease an' Beans, et een or morn,
    Perfume the plain,
Leeze me on thee *John Barleycorn*,
    Thou king o' grain !

On thee aft Scotland chows her cood,
In souple scones, the wale o' food !
Or tumblin in the boiling flood !
    Wi' kail an' beef ;
But when thou pours thy strong *heart's blood*,
    There thou shines chief.

Food fills the wame, an' keeps us livin ;
Tho' life's a gift no worth receivin,
When heavy-dragg'd wi' pine an' grievin ;
    But oil'd by thee,
The wheels o' life gae down-hill, scrievin,
    Wi' rattlin glee.

Thou clears the head o' doited Lear:
Thou chears the heart o' drooping Care;
Thou strings the nerves o' Labor-sair,
        At 's weary toil;
Thou even brightens dark Despair
        Wi' gloomy smile.

Aft, clad in massy, siller weed,
Wi' Gentles thou erects thy head;
Yet humbly kind, in time o' need,
        The *poor man's* wine,
His wee drap pirratch, or his bread,
        Thou kitchens fine.

Thou art the life o' public haunts;
But thee, what were our fairs and rants?
Ev'n godly meetings o' the saunts,
        By thee inspir'd,
When gaping they besiege the *tents*,
        Are doubly fir'd.

That *merry night* we get the corn in!
O sweetly, then, thou reams the horn in!
Or reekan on a New-Year-mornin
        In cog or bicker,
An' just a wee drap *sp'ritual burn* in,
        An' gusty sucker!

When Vulcan gies his bellys breath,
An' ploughmen gather wi' their graith,
O rare ! to see thee fizz an' freath
        I' th' lugget caup !
Then *Burnewin* comes on like Death
        At ev'ry chap.

Nae mercy, then, for airn or steel ;
The brawnie, banie, ploughman-chiel,
Brings hard owrehip, wi' sturdy wheel,
        The strong forehammer,
Till block an' studdie ring an' reel
        Wi' dinsome clamour.

When skirlin weanies see the light,
Thou maks the gossips clatter bright,
How fumblin' coofs their dearies slight,
        Wae worth them for't !
While healths gae round to him wha, tight,
        Gies famous sport.

When neebors anger at a plea,
An' just as wud as wud can be,
How easy can the *barley-brie*
        Cement the quarrel !
It's aye the cheapest Lawyer's fee,
        To taste the barrel.

Alake! that e'er my *Muse* has reason
To wyte her countrymen wi' treason!
But monie daily weet their weason
           Wi' liquors nice,
An' hardly, in a winter's season,
           E'er spier her price.

Wae worth that *Brandy*, burnan trash!
Fell source o' monie a pain an' brash!
Twins monie a poor, doylt, druken hash,
           O' half his days;
An' sends, beside, auld *Scotland's* cash
           To her warst faes.

Ye Scots, wha wish auld Scotland well,
Ye chief, to you my tale I tell,
Poor plackless devils like mysel
           It sets you ill,
Wi' bitter, dearthfu' *wines* to mell,
           Or foreign gill.

May *Gravels* round his blather wrench,
An' *Gouts* torment him, inch by inch,
Wha twists his gruntle wi' a glunch
           O' sour disdain,
Out owre a glass o' *Whisky-punch*
           Wi' honest men!

O *Whisky!* soul o' plays an' pranks!
Accept a *Bardie's* gratefu' thanks!
When wanting thee, what tuneless cranks
      Are my poor Verses!
Thou comes——they rattle i' their ranks
      At ither's arses!

Thee, *Ferintosh!* O sadly lost!
Scotland lament frae coast to coast!
Now collic-grips, an barkin hoast,
      May kill us a';
For loyal Forbes' *Charter'd boast*
      Is ta'en awa!

Thae curst horse-leeches o' th' Excise,
Wha mak the *Whisky stells* their prize!
Haud up thy han' Deil! ance, twice, *thrice!*
      There, seize the blinkers!
An' bake them up in brunstane pies
      For poor damn'd drinkers.

Fortune! if thou'll but gie me still
Hale breeks, a scone, an' *whisky gill,*
An' rowth o' *rhyme* to rave at will,
      Tak' a' the rest,
An' deal't about as thy blind skill
      Directs thee best.

THE HOLY FAIR.

UPON a simmer Sunday morn,
    When Nature's face is fair,
I walked forth to view the corn,
    An' snuff the callor air.
The risin' sun, owre GALSTON Muirs,
    Wi' glorious light was glintan;
The hares were hirplan down the furrs,
    The lav'rocks they were chantan
              Fu' sweet that day.

As lightsomely I glowr'd abroad,
    To see a scene sae gay,
Three *hizzies*, early at the road,
    Cam skelpan up the way.
Twa had manteeles o' dolefu' black,
    But ane wi' lyart lining;
The third, that gaed a wee a-back,
    Was in the fashion shining
              Fu' gay that day.

The *twa* appear'd like sisters twin,
    In feature, form, an' claes;

Their visage wither'd, lang an' thin,
    An' sour as ony slaes:
The *third* cam up, hap-step-an'-lowp,
    As light as ony lambie,
An' wi' a curchie low did stoop,
    As soon as e'er she saw me,
              Fu' kind that day.

Wi' bonnet aff, quoth I, "Sweet lass,
    I think ye seem to ken me;
I'm sure I've seen that bonie face,
    But yet I canna name ye."
Quo' she, an' laughan as she spak,
    An' taks me by the han's,
"Ye, for my sake, hae gi'en the feck
    Of a' the *ten comman's*
              A screed some day.

" My name is FUN—your cronie dear,
    The nearest friend ye hae;
An' this is SUPERSTITION here,
    An' that's HYPOCRISY.
I'm gaun to * * * holy fair,
    To spend an hour in daffin:
Gin ye'll go there, yon runkl'd pair,
    We will get famous laughin
              At them this day."

Quoth I, "With a' my heart, I'll do't ;
   I'll get my sunday's sark on,
An' meet you on the holy spot ;
   Faith, we'se hae fine remarkin !"
Then I gaed hame at crowdie-time,
   An' soon I made me ready ;
For roads were clad, frae side to side,
   Wi' monie a wearie bodie,
                    In droves that day.

Here, farmers gash, in ridin graith,
   Gaed hoddan by their cotters ;
There, swankies young, in braw braid-claith,
   Are springan owre the gutters.
The lasses, skelpan barefit, thrang,
   In silks an' scarlets glitter ;
Wi' *sweet-milk cheese*, in monie a whang,
   An' *farls*, bak'd wi' butter,
                    Fu' crump that day.

When by the *plate* we set our nose,
   Weel heaped up wi' ha'pence,
A greedy glowr *black-bonnet* throws,
   ' An' we maun draw our tippence.
Then in we go to see the show,
   On ev'ry side they're gath'ran,

Some carryin dails, some chairs an' stools,
   An' some are busy bleth'rin
            Right loud that day.

Here stands a shed to fend the show'rs,
   An' screen our countra Gentry ;
There, *racer Jess*, an' twa-three whores,
   Are blinkin at the entry.
Here sits a raw o' tittlin jads,
   Wi' heaving breasts an' bare neck,
An' there, a batch o' Wabster lads,
   Blackguarding frae Kilmarnock
            For fun this day.

Here, some are thinkan on their sins,
   An' some upo' their claes ;
Ane curses feet that fyl'd his shins,
   Anither sighs an' prays :
On this hand sits an Elect swatch,
   Wi' screw'd-up, grace-proud faces ;
On that, a set o' chaps, at watch,
   Thrang winkan on the lasses
            To *chairs* that day.

O happy is that man, an' blest !
   Nae wonder that it pride him !
Whase ain dear lass, that he likes best,
   Comes clinkan down beside him !

Wi' arm repos'd on the *chair-back*,
 He sweetly does compose him ;
Which, by degrees, slips round her *neck*,
 An's loof upon her bosom
     Unkend that day.

Now a' the congregation o'er
 In silent expectation ;
For M * * * speels the holy door,
 Wi' tidings o' salvation.
Should *Hornie*, as in ancient days,
 'Mang sons o' G— present him,
The vera sight o' M * * * face,
 To's ain *het hame* had sent him
     Wi' fright that day.

Hear how he clears the points o' Faith
 Wi' rattlin an' wi' thumpin !
Now meekly calm, now wild in wrath,
 He's stampan an' he's jumpan !
His lengthen'd chin, his turned-up snout,
 His eldritch squeel an' gestures,
O how they fire the heart devout,
 Like *cantharidian* plasters,
     On sic a day !

But, hark ! the *tent* has chang'd it's voice ;
 There's peace an' rest nae langer :

For a' the *real judges* rise,
   They canna sit for anger,
* * * opens out his cauld harangues,
   On *practice* and on *morals;*
An' aff the *godly* pour in thrangs,
   To gie the jars an' barrels
               A lift that day.

What signifies his barren shine
   Of *moral pow'rs* an' *reason?*
His English style, an' gesture fine,
   Are a' clean out o' season.
Like SOCRATES or ANTONINE,
   Or some auld pagan Heathen,
The *moral man* he does define,
   But ne'er a word o' *faith* in
               That's right that day.

In guid time comes an antidote
   Against sic pooson'd nostrum;
For * * *, frae the water-fit,
   Ascends the *holy rostrum:*
See, up he's got the word o' God
   An' meek an' mim has view'd it,
While COMMON-SENSE has ta'en the road,
   An' aff, an' up the Cowgate
               Fast, fast, that day.

Wee * * *, neist, the Guard relieves,
   An' Orthodoxy raibles,
Tho' in his heart he weel believes,
   An' thinks it auld wives' fables :
But, faith ! the birkie wants a *Manse*,
   So, cannilie he hums them ;
Altho' his *carnal* Wit an' Sense
   Like hafflins-wise o'ercomes him
                  At times that day

Now, butt an' ben, the Change-house fills,
   Wi' *yill-caup* Commentators :
Here's crying out for bakes an' gills,
   An' there the pint-stowp clatters ;
While thick an' thrang, an' loud an' lang,
   Wi' *Logic*, an' wi' *Scripture*,
They raise a din, that in the end
   Is like to breed a rupture
                  O' wrath that day.

Leeze me on Drink ! it gi'es us mair
   Than either School or College :
It kindles Wit, it waukens Lair,
   It pangs us fou o' Knowledge.
Be't *whisky-gill*, or *penny-wheep*,
   Or ony stronger potion,

It never fails, on drinkin' deep,
　　To kittle up our *notion*
　　　　　　By night or day.

The lads an' lasses, blythely bent
　　To mind baith *saul* an' *body*,
Sit round the table, weel content,
　　An' steer about the *toddy*.
On this ane's dress, an' that ane's leuk,
　　They're makin' observations;
While some are cozie i' the neuk,
　　An' formin *assignations*
　　　　　　To meet some day.

But now the Lord's ain trumpet touts,
　　Till a' the hills are rairan,
An' echoes back return the shouts;
　　Black * * * is na spairan:
His piercing words, like Highlan swords,
　　Divide the joints an' marrow;
His talk of Hell, whare devils dwell,
　　Our vera "Sauls does harrow"
　　　　　　Wi' fright that day!

A vast, unbottom'd boundless *Pit*,
　　Fill'd fou of lowan brunstane,
Whase ragin flame, an' scorchin heat,
　　Wad melt the hardest whun-stane,

The half-asleep start up wi' fear,
  An' think they hear it roaran,
When presently it does appear,
  'Twas but some neebor snoran
                Asleep that day.

'Twad be owre lang a tale to tell
  How monie stories past,
An' how they crowded to the yill,
  When they were a' dismist:
How drink gaed round, in cogs an' caups,
  Amang the furms and benches;
An' *cheese* an' *bread*, frae women's laps,
  Was dealt about in lunches,
                An' dawds that day.

In comes a gaucie, gash *Guidwife*,
  An' sits down by the fire,
Syne draws her *kebbuck* an' her knife;
  The lasses they are shyer.
The auld *Guidmen*, about the *grace*,
  Frae side to side they bother,
Till some ane by his bonnet lays,
  An' gies them't like a *tether*,
                Fu' lang that day.

Waesucks! for him that gets nae lass,
  Or lasses that hae naething!

Sma' need has he to say a grace,
  Or melvie his braw claithing !
O *Wives*, be mindfu', ance yoursel
  How bonie lads ye wanted,
An' dinna, for a *kebbuck-heel*,
  Let lasses be affronted
           On sic a day !

Now *Clinkumbell*, wi' rattlan tow,
  Begins to jow an' croon ;
Some swagger hame, the best they dow,
  Some wait the afternoon.
At slaps the billies halt a blink,
  Till lasses strip their shoon :
Wi' *faith* an' *hope*, an' *love* an' *drink*,
  They're a' in famous tune
           For crack that day.

How monie hearts this day converts
  O' sinners and o' Lasses !
Their hearts o' stane, gin night, are gane
  As saft as ony flesh is.
There's some are fou o' *love divine*,
  There's some are fou o' *brandy ;*
An' monie jobs that day begin,
  May end in *Houghmagandie*
           Some ither day.

THE BRIGS OF AYR.

A POEM.

INSCRIBED TO JOHN BALLANTINE, ESQ., AYR.

THE simple Bard, rough at the rustic plough,
Learning his tuneful trade from ev'ry bough;
The chanting linnet or the mellow thrush,
Hailing the setting sun, sweet, in the green thorn bush,
The soaring lark, the perching red-breast shrill,
Or deep-ton'd plovers, grey, wild-whistling o'er the hill;
Shall he, nurst in the Peasant's lowly shed,
To hardy Independence bravely bred,
By early Poverty to hardship steel'd,
And train'd to arms in stern Misfortune's field,
Shall he be guilty of their hireling crimes,
The servile, mercenary Swiss of rhymes?
Or labour hard the panegyric close,
With all the venal soul of dedicating Prose?
No! though his artless strains he rudely sings,
And throws his hand uncouthly o'er the strings,
He glows with all the spirit of the Bard,
Fame, honest Fame, his great, his dear reward.
Still, if some Patron's gen'rous care he trace,
Skill'd in the secret, to bestow with grace;

When B * * * befriends his humble name
And hands the rustic Stranger up to fame,
With heartfelt throes his grateful bosom swells,
The god-like bliss, to give, alone excels.

'Twas when the stacks get on their winter-hap,
And thack and rape secure the toil-won crap;
Potatoe-bings are snugged up frae skaith
Of coming Winter's biting, frosty breath;
The bees, rejoicing o'er their summer-toils,
Unnumber'd buds and flow'rs delicious spoils,
Seal'd up with frugal care in massive, waxen piles,
Are doom'd by Man, that tyrant o'er the weak,
The death o' devils, smoor'd wi' brimstone reek :
The thund'ring guns are heard on ev'ry side,
The wounded coveys, reeling, scatter wide;
The feather'd field-mates, bound by Nature's tie,
Sires, mothers, children, in one carnage lie :
(What warm, poetic heart, but inly bleeds,
And execrates man's savage, ruthless deeds!)
Nae mair the flow'r in field or meadow springs;
Nae mair the grove with airy concert rings,
Except perhaps the Robin's whistling glee,
Proud o' the height o' some bit half-lang tree :
The hoary morn precede the sunny days,
Mild, calm, serene, wide-spreads the noontide blaze,
While thick the gossamour waves wanton in the rays.

'Twas in that season; when a simple Bard,
Unknown and poor, simplicity's reward,
Ae night, within the ancient brugh of *Ayr*,
By whim inspir'd, or haply prest wi' care,
He left his bed and took his wayward rout,
And down by *Simpson's* wheel'd the left about:
(Whether impell'd by all-directing Fate,
To witness what I after shall narrate;
Or whether, rapt in meditation high,
He wandered out he knew not where nor why:)
The drowsy *Dungeon-clock* had number'd two,
And *Wallace-Tow'r* had sworn the fact was true:
The tide-swoln Firth, wi' sullen-sounding roar,
Through the still night dash'd hoarse along the shore:
All else was hush'd as Nature's closed ee;
The silent moon shone high o'er tow'r and tree:
The chilly Frost, beneath the silver beam,
Crept, gently-crusting, owre the glittering stream.—

When, lo! on either hand the list'ning Bard,
The clanging sugh of whistling wings is heard;
Two dusky forms dart thro' the midnight air,
Swift as the Gos drives on the wheeling hare;
Ane on th' *Auld Brig* his airy shape uprears,
The ither flutters o'er the *rising piers:*
Our warlock Rhymer instantly descry'd
The Sprites that owre the *Brigs of Ayr* preside.

(That Bards are second-sighted is nae joke,
And ken the lingo of the sp'ritual folk;
Fays, Spunkies, Kelpies, a', they can explain them,
And ev'n the vera deils they brawly ken them.)
Auld Brig appear'd o' ancient Pictish race,
The vera wrinkles Gothic in his face:
He seem'd as he wi' time had warstl'd lang,
Yet, teughly doure, he bade an unco bang.
New Brig was buskit in a braw, new coat,
That he, at Lon'on, from ane *Adams* got;
In's hand five taper staves as smooth's a bead,
Wi' virls an' whirlygigums at the head.
The Goth was stalking round with anxious search,
Spying the time-worn flaws in ev'ry arch;
It chanc'd his new-come neebor took his e'e,
And e'en a vex'd and angry heart had he!
Wi' thieveless sneer to see his modish mien,
He, down the water, gies him this guid-een——

AULD BRIG.

I doubt na, frien', ye'll think ye're nae sheep-shank,
Ance ye were streekit owre frae bank to bank!
But gin ye be a Brig as auld as me,
Tho', faith, that date, I doubt, ye'll never see;
There'll be, if that day come, I'll wad a boddle,
Some fewer whigmeleeries in your noddle.

NEW BRIG.

Auld Vandal, ye but shew your little mense,
Just much about it wi' your scanty sense;
Will your poor, narrow foot-path of a street,
Where twa wheel-barrows tremble when they meet,
Your ruin'd, formless bulk of stane and lime,
Compare wi' bonie *Brigs* o' modern time?
There's men of taste wou'd tak the *Ducat-stream*,
Tho' they should cast the vera sark and swim,
Ere they would grate their feelings wi' the view
O' sic an ugly Gothic hulk as you.

AULD BRIG.

Conceited gowk! puff'd up wi' windy pride!
This mony a year I've stood the flood an' tide;
And tho' wi' crazy eild I'm sair forfairn,
I'll be a *Brig*, when ye're a shapeless cairn!
As yet ye little ken about the matter,
But twa-three winters will inform ye better.
When heavy, dark, continued, a'-day rains
Wi' deepening deluges o'erflow the plains;
When from the hills where springs the brawling *Coil*,
Or stately *Lugar's* mossy fountains boil,
Or where the *Greenock* winds his moorland course,
Or haunted *Garpal* draws his feeble source,
Arous'd by blustering winds an' spotting thowes,
In mony a torrent down his snaw-broo rowes;

While crashing ice, borne on the roaring speat
Sweeps dams, an' mills, an' brigs, a' to the gate;
And from *Glenbuck,* down to the *Ratton-key,*
Auld *Ayr* is just one lengthen'd, tumbling sea;
Then down ye'll hurl, deil nor ye never rise!
And dash the gumlie jaups up to the pouring skies,
A lesson sadly teaching, to your cost,
That Architecture's noble art is lost!

NEW BRIG.

Fine *architecture,* trowth, I needs must say't o't!
The Lord be thankit that we've tint the gate o't!
Gaunt, ghastly, ghaist-alluring edifices,
Hanging with threat'ning jut like precipices:
O'er-arching, mouldy, gloom-inspiring coves,
Supporting roofs, fantastic, stony groves:
Windows and doors in nameless sculptures drest,
With order, symmetry, or taste unblest;
Forms like some bedlam Statuary's dream,
The craz'd creations of misguided whim;
Forms might be worshipp'd on the bended knee,
And still the *second dread command* be free,
Their likeness is not found on earth, in air, or sea.
Mansions that would disgrace the building-taste
Of any mason reptile, bird, or beast;
Fit only for a doited Monkish race,
Or frosty maids forsworn the dear embrace,

Or Cuifs of later times, wha held the notion,
That sullen gloom was Sterling true devotion;
Fancies that our guid Burgh denies protection,
And soon may they expire, unblest with resurrection!

AULD BRIG.

O ye, my dear-remember'd, ancient yealins,
Were ye but here to share my wounded feelings!
Ye worthy *Proveses*, an' mony a *Bailie*,
Wha in the paths o' righteousness did toil ay;
Ye dainty *Deacons*, an' ye douce *Conveeners*,
To whom our moderns are but causey-cleaners;
Ye godly Councils, wha hae blest this town;
Ye godly *Brethren* o' the sacred gown,
Wha meekly gae your *hurdies* to the *smiters;*
And (what would now be strange) ye *godly Writers:*
A' ye douce folk I've borne aboon the broo,
Were ye but here, what would ye say or do!
How would your spirits groan in deep vexation,
To see each melancholy alteration;
And, agonizing, curse the time and place
When ye begat the base, degen'rate race!
Nae langer Rev'rend Men, their country's glory,
In plain braid Scots hold forth a plain braid story:
Nae langer thrifty Citizens, an' douce,
Meet owre a pint, or in the Council-house;
But staumrel, corky-headed, graceless Gentry,

The herryment and ruin of the country;
Men, three-parts made by Taylors and by Barbers,
Wha waste your weel-hain'd gear on damned *new Brigs*
    and *Harbours!*

NEW BRIG.

Now haud you there! for faith ye've said enough,
And muckle mair than ye can mak to through.
As for your Priesthood, I shall say but little,
Corbies and *Clergy* are a shot right kittle:
But, under favour o' your langer beard,
Abuse o' Magistrates might weel be spar'd:
To liken them to your auld-warld squad,
I must needs say, comparisons are odd.
In *Ayr*, Wag-wits nae mair can have a handle
To mouth 'a Citizen,' a term o' scandal:
Nae mair the Council waddles down the street,
In all the pomp of ignorant conceit;
Men wha grew wise priggin owre hops an' raisins,
Or gather'd lib'ral views in Bonds and Seisins.
If haply Knowledge, on a random tramp,
Had shor'd them wi' a glimmer of his lamp,
And would to Common-sense for once betray'd them,
Plain, dull Stupidity stept kindly in to aid them.

What farther clishmaclaver might been said,
What bloody wars, if Sprites had blood to shed,

No man can tell; but, all before their sight
A fairy train appear'd in order bright:
Adown the glittering stream they featly danc'd;
Bright to the moon their various dresses glanc'd:
They footed o'er the wat'ry glass so neat,
The infant ice scarce bent beneath their feet:
While arts of Minstrelsy among them rung,
And soul-ennobling Bards heroic ditties sung.

O had *M'Lauchlan*, thairm-inspiring Sage,
Been there to hear this heavenly band engage,
When thro' his dear Strathspeys they bore with Highland
    rage,
Or when they struck old Scotia's melting airs,
The lover's raptur'd joys or bleeding cares;
How would his Highland lug been nobler fir'd,
And ev'n his matchless hand with finer touch inspir'd!
No guest could tell what instrument appear'd,
But all the soul of Music's self was heard;
Harmonious concert rung in every part,
While simple melody pour'd moving on the heart.

The Genius of the Stream in front appears,
A venerable Chief advanc'd in years;
His hoary head with water-lilies crown'd,
His manly leg with garter tangle bound.
Next came the loveliest pair in all the ring,

Sweet Female Beauty hand in hand with Spring;
Then, crown'd with flow'ry hay, came Rural Joy,
And Summer with his fervid-beaming eye:
All-cheering Plenty, with her flowing horn,
Led yellow Autumn wreath'd with nodding corn;
Then Winter's time-bleach'd locks did hoary show,
By Hospitality with cloudless brow.
Next followed Courage with his martial stride,
From where the *Feal* wild-woody coverts hide;
Benevolence, with mild, benignant air,
A female form, came from the tow'rs of *Stair:*
Learning and Worth in equal measures trode,
From simple *Catrine*, their long-lov'd abode:
Last, white-rob'd Peace, crown'd with a hazle wreath,
To rustic Agriculture did bequeath
The broken, iron instruments of Death:
At sight of whom our Sprites forgat their kindling wrath.

ADDRESS TO THE DEIL.

"O Prince! O Chief of many throned Pow'rs,
That led th' embattled Seraphim to war—"
MILTON.

O THOU! whatever title suit thee,
   Auld Hornie, Satan, Nick, or Clootie,
Wha in yon cavern grim an' sootie,
       Clos'd under hatches,
Spairges about the brunstane cootie,
       To scaud poor wretches!

Hear me, *auld Hangie*, for a wee,
An' let poor *damned bodies* be;
I'm sure sma' pleasure it can gie,
       Ev'n to a *deil*,
To skelp an' scaud poor dogs like me,
       An' hear us squeel!

Great is thy pow'r, an' great thy fame;
Far kend an' noted is thy name;
An' tho' yon *lowan heugh*'s thy hame,
       Thou travels far;
An' faith! thou's neither lag nor lame,
       Nor blate nor scaur.

Whyles, rangin like a roaran lion
For prey, a' holes an' corners tryin;
Whyles, on the strong-wing'd Tempest flyin,
      Tirlan the kirks;
Whyles, in the human bosom pryin,
      Unseen thou lurks.

I've heard my reverend *Graunie* say,
In lanely glens ye like to stray;
Or where auld, ruin'd castles, gray,
      Nod to the moon,
Ye fright the nightly wand'rer's way,
      Wi' eldritch croon.

When twilight did my graunie summon,
To say her pray'rs, douce, honest woman!
Aft yont the dyke she's heard you bumman
      Wi' eerie drone;
Or, rustlin, thro' the boortries comin,
      Wi' heavy groan.

Ae dreary, windy, winter night,
The stars shot down wi' sklentan light,
Wi' you, *mysel*, I gat a fright,
      Ayont the lough;
Ye, like a *rash-buss*, stood in sight,
      Wi' waving sugh.

The cudgel in my nieve did shake,
Each bristl'd hair stood like a stake,
When wi' an eldritch, stoor *quaick, quaick,*
   Amang the springs,
Awa ye squatter'd like a *drake,*
   On whistling wings.

Let *Warlocks* grim, an' wither'd *Hags,*
Tell how wi' you on ragweed nags,
They skim the muirs an dizzy crags,
   Wi' wicked speed;
And in kirk-yards renew their leagues,
   Owre howkit dead.

Thence, countra wives, wi' toil an' pain,
May plunge an' plunge the *kirn* in vain;
For, Oh! the yellow treasure's taen
   By witching skill;
An' dawtet, twal-pint *Hawkie's* gain
   As yell's the Bill.

Thence, mystic knots mak great abuse,
On *Young-Guidmen,* fond, keen, an' croose;
When the best wark-lume i' the house,
   By cantraip wit,
Is instant made no worth a louse,
   Just at the bit.

When thawes disolve the snawy hoord,
An' float the jinglan icy-boord,
Then *Water-kelpies* haunt the foord,
   By your direction,
An' nighted Trav'llers are allur'd
   To their destruction.

An' aft your moss-traversing Spunkies
Decoy the wight that late an' drunk is:
The bleezan, curst, mischievous monkies
   Delude his eyes,
Till in some miry slough he sunk is,
   Ne'er mair to rise.

When MASONS' mystic *word* an' *grip*,
In storms an' tempests raise you up,
Some cock or cat your rage maun stop,
   Or, strange to tell!
The *youngest Brother* ye wad whip
   Aff straught to hell.

Lang syne, in EDEN'S bonie yard,
When youthfu' lovers first were pair'd,
An' all the Soul of Love they shar'd,
   The raptur'd hour,
Sweet on the fragrant, flow'ry swaird,
   In shady bow'r.

Then you, ye auld, snick-drawing dog !
Ye came to Paradise incog,
An' play'd on man a cursed brogue,
   (Black be you fa !)
An' gied the infant warld a shog,
   'Maist ruin'd a'.

D'ye mind that day, when in a bizz,
Wi' reeket duds, an' reestet gizz,
Ye did present your smoutie phiz,
   'Mang better folk,
An' sklented on the *man of Uzz*
   Your spitefu' joke?

An' how ye gat him i' your thrall,
An' brak him out o' house an' hal',
While scabs an' botches did him gall,
   Wi' bitter clew,
An' lows'd his ill-tongu'd, wicked *Scawl*,
   Was warst ava?

But a' your doings to rehearse,
Your wily snares an' fechtin fierce,
Sin' that day MICHAEL did you pierce,
   Down to this time,
Wad ding a' *Lallan* tongue, or *Erse*,
   In Prose or Rhyme.

An' now, auld *Cloots*, I ken ye're thinkan,
A certain *Bardie's* rantan, drinkan,
Some luckless hour will send him linkan,
   To your black pit;
But faith! he'll turn a corner jinkan,
   An' cheat you yet.

But, fare you weel, auld *Nickie-ben*
O wad ye tak a thought an' men'!
Ye aiblins might—I dinna ken—
   Still hae a *stake*—
I'm wae to think upo' yon den,
   Ev'n for your sake!

THE VISION.

DUAN FIRST.

THE sun had closed the *winter-day*,
 The Curlers quat their roaring play,
An' hunger'd Maukin taen her way
   To kail-yards green,
While faithless snaws ilk step betray
   Whare she has been.

The thresher's weary *flingin-tree*,
The lee-lang day had tir'd me;
And whan the Day had clos'd his e'e,
    Far i' the West,
Ben i' the *Spence*, right pensivelie,
    I gaed to rest.

There, lanely, by the ingle-cheek,
I sat and ey'd the spewing reek,
That fill'd, wi' hoast-provoking smeek,
    The auld, clay biggin;
An' heard the restless rattons squeak
    About the riggin.

All in this mottie, misty clime,
I backward mus'd on wasted time,
How I had spent my *youthfu' prime*,
    An' done nae-thing,
But stringing blethers up in rhyme,
    For fools to sing.

Had I to guid advice but harket,
I might, by this, hae led a market,
Or strutted in a Bank, and clarket
    My Cash-Account:
While here, half-mad, half-fed, half-sarket,
    Is a' th' amount.

I started, mutt'ring blockhead ! coof !
And heav'd on high my wauket loof,
To swear by a' yon starry roof,
          Or some rash aith,
That I, henceforth, would be *rhyme-proof*
          Till my last breath—

When click ! the *string* the *snick* did draw ;
And jee ! the door gaed to the wa' ;
And by my ingle-lowe I saw,
          Now bleezan bright,
A tight, outlandish *Hizzie*, braw,
          Come full in sight.

Ye need na doubt, I held my whisht ;
The infant aith, half-form'd, was crusht ;
I glowr'd as eerie's I'd been dusht
          In some wild glen ;
When sweet, like *modest Worth*, she blusht,
          And stepped ben.

Green, slender, leaf-clad Holly-boughs
Were twisted, gracefu', round her brows,
I took her for some SCOTTISH MUSE,
          By that same token ;
And come to stop these reckless vows,
          Would soon been broken.

A "hair-brain'd, sentimental trace,"
Was strongly marked in her face;
A wildly-witty, rustic grace
   Shone full upon her;
Her *eye*, ev'n turn'd on empty space,
   Beam'd keen with *Honor*.

Down flow'd her robe, a tartar sheen,
Till half a leg was scrimply seen;
And such a *leg!* my BESS, I ween,
   Could only peer it;
Sae straught, sae taper, tight and clean,
   Nane else came near it.

Her Mantle large, of greenish hue,
My gazing wonder chiefly drew;
Deep *lights* and *shades*, bold-mingling, threw
   A lustre grand;
And seem'd, to my astonish'd view
   A *well-known* Land.

Here, rivers in the sea were lost;
There, mountains to the skies were tost:
Here, tumbling billows mark'd the coast,
   With surging foam;
There, distant shone, *Art's* lofty boast,
   The lordly dome.

Here, DOON pour'd down his far-fetch'd floods;
There, well-fed IRWINE stately thuds,
Auld hermit AIRE staw thro' his woods,
   On to the shore;
And many a lesser torrent scuds,
   With seeming roar.

Low, in a sandy valley spread,
An ancient BOROUGH rear'd her head;
Still, as in *Scottish Story* read,
   She boasts a *Race*,
To ev'ry nobler virtue bred,
   And polish'd grace.

DUAN SECOND.

WITH musing-deep, astonish'd stare,
I view'd the heavenly-seeming *Fair;*
A whisp'ring *throb* did witness bear,
   Of kindred sweet,
When with an elder Sister's air
   She did me greet.

"All hail! *my own* inspired Bard!
In me thy native Muse regard!
Nor longer mourn thy fate is hard,
   Thus poorly low!
I come to give thee such *reward*
   As *we* bestow.

" Know, the great *Genius* of this Land
Has many a light, aërial band,
Who, all beneath his high command,
   Harmoniously,
As *Arts* or *Arms* they understand,
   Their labors ply.

" They SCOTIA'S Race among them share :
Some fire the Sodger on to dare ;
Some rouse the *Patriot* up to bare
   Corruption's heart :
Some teach the *Bard*, a darling care,
   The tuneful Art.

"'Mong swelling floods of reeking gore,
They ardent, kindling spirits pour ;
Or, 'mid the venal Senate's roar,
   They, sightless, stand,
To mend the honest *Patriot-lore*,
   And grace the hand.

" Hence, FULLARTON, the brave and young ;
Hence, DEMPSTER'S truth-prevailing tongue ;
Hence, sweet harmonious BEATTIE sung
   His " Minstrel lays ;"
Or tore, with noble ardour stung,
   The *Sceptic's* bays.

" To lower Orders are assign'd,
The humbler ranks of Human-kind,
The rustic Bard, the lab'ring Hind,
             The Artisan ;
All chuse, as, various they're inclin'd,
             The various man.

" When yellow waves the heavy grain,
The threat'ning Storm some, strongly, rein ;
Some teach to meliorate the plain,
             With *tillage-skill ;*
And some instruct the Shepherd-train,
             Blythe o'er the hill.

" Some hint the Lover's harmless wile ;
Some grace the Maiden's artless smile ;
Some soothe the Lab'rer's weary toil,
             For humble gains,
And make his *cottage-scenes* beguile
             His cares and pains.

" Some, bounded to a district-space,
Explore at large Man's *infant race,*
To mark the embryotic trace
             Of *rustic Bard ;*
And careful note each op'ning grace,
             A guide and guard.

" *Of these am I*—COILA my name;
And this district as mine I claim,
Where once the *Campbells*, chiefs of fame,
   Held ruling pow'r:
I mark'd thy embryo-tuneful flame,
   Thy natal hour.

"With future hope, I oft would gaze,
Fond, on thy little, early ways,
Thy rudely-caroll'd, chiming phrase,
   In uncouth rhymes,
Fir'd at the simple, artless lays
   Of other times.

" I saw thee seek the sounding shore,
Delighted with the dashing roar;
Or when the *North* his fleecy store
   Drove thro' the sky,
I saw grim nature's visage hoar
   Struck thy young eye.

"Or when the deep-green-mantl'd Earth
Warm-cherish'd ev'ry flow'ret's birth,
And joy and music pouring forth
   In ev'ry grove,
I saw thee eye the gen'ral mirth
   With boundless love.

"When ripen'd fields, and azure skies,
Call'd forth the *Reaper's* rustling noise,
I saw thee leave their ev'ning joys,
   And lonely stalk,
To vent thy bosom's swelling rise
   In pensive walk.

"When *youthful Love*, warm-blushing, strong,
Keen-shivering shot thy nerves along,
Those accents, grateful to thy tongue,
   Th' adored *Name*,
I taught thee how to pour in song,
   To soothe thy flame.

"I saw thy pulse's maddening play,
Wild-send thee Pleasure's devious way,
Misled by Fancy's *meteor-ray*,
   By Passion driven;
But yet the *light* that led astray
   Was *light* from Heaven.

"I taught thy manners-painting strains,
The *loves*, the *ways* of simple swains,
Till now, o'er all my wide domains,
   Thy fame extends;
And some, the pride of *Coila's* plains,
   Become thy friends.

" Thou canst not learn, nor can I show,
To paint with *Thomson's* landscape-glow ;
Or wake the bosom-melting throe,
    With *Shenstone's* art ;
Or pour, with *Gray*, the moving flow,
    Warm on the heart.

" Yet, all beneath th' unrivall'd Rose,
The lowly Daisy sweetly blows ;
Tho' large the forest's Monarch throws
    His army shade,
Yet green the juicy Hawthorn grows,
    Adown the glade.

" Then never murmur nor repine ;
Strive in thy *humble sphere* to shine ;
And trust me, not *Potosi's mine*,
    Nor *King's regard*,
Can give a bliss o'ermatching thine,
    A *rustic Bard*.

" To give my counsels all in one,
Thy *tuneful flame* still careful fan ;
Preserve *the dignity of Man*,
    With Soul erect ;
And trust, the UNIVERSAL PLAN
    Will all protect.

"*And wear thou this*"—she solemn said,
And bound the *Holly* round my head :
The polish'd leaves, and berries red,
   Did rustling play ;
And, like a passing thought, she fled
   In light away.

ADDRESS TO THE UNCO GUID, OR THE RIGIDLY RIGHTEOUS.

My son, these maxims make a rule,
 And lump them aye thegither;
The Rigid Righteous is a fool,
 The Rigid Wise anither :
The cleanest corn that e'er was dight,
 May hae some pyles o' caff in;
So ne'er a fellow-creature slight
 For random fits o' daffin.
     SOLOMON—Eccles. vii. 16.

O YE wha are sae guid yoursel,
 Sae pious and sae holy,
Ye've nought to do but mark and tell
 Your Neebour's fauts and folly !
Whase life is like a weel-gaun mill,
 Supply'd wi' store o' water,
The heapet happer's ebbing still,
 And still the clap plays clatter.

Hear me, ye venerable Core,
  As counsel for poor mortals,
That frequent pass douce Wisdom's door,
  For glaikit Folly's portals;
I, for their thoughtless, careless sakes,
  Would here propone defences,
Their donsie tricks, their black mistakes,
  Their failings and mischances.

Ye see your state wi' their's compar'd,
  And shudder at the niffer,
But cast a moment's fair regard,
  What maks the mighty differ;
Discount what scant occasion gave
  That purity ye pride in,
And (what's aft mair than a' the lave)
  Your better art o' hiding.

Think, when your castigated pulse
  Gies now and then a wallop,
What raging must his veins convulse,
  That still eternal gallop:
Wi' wind and tide fair i' your tail,
  Right on ye scud your sea-way;
But, in the teeth o' baith to sail,
  It maks an unco leeway.

See Social life and Glee sit down,
    All joyous and unthinking,
Till, quite transmugrify'd, they're grown
    Debauchery and Drinking :
O would they stay to calculate
    Th' eternal consequences ;
Or your more dreaded hell to state,
    Damnation of expenses !

Ye high, exalted, virtuous Dames,
    Ty'd up in godly laces,
Before ye gie poor *Frailty* names,
    Suppose a change o' cases ;
A dear-lov'd lad, convenience snug,
    A treacherous inclination—
But, let me whisper i' your lug,
    Ye're aiblins nae temptation.

Then gently scan your brother Man,
    Still gentler sister woman ;
Tho' they may gang a-kennin wrang,
    To step aside is human :
One point must still be greatly dark,
    The moving *Why* they do it ;
And just as lamely can ye mark,
    How far perhaps they rue it.

Who made the heart, 'tis *He* alone
  Decidedly can try us,
He knows each chord its various tone,
  Each spring its various bias:
Then at the balance let's be mute,
  We never can adjust it;
What's *done* we partly may compute,
  But know not what's *resisted*.

HALLOWEEN.

Yes! let the Rich deride, the Proud disdain,
The simple pleasures of the lowly train;
To me more dear, congenial to my heart,
One native charm, than all the gloss of art.
                                GOLDSMITH.

UPON that *night*, when Fairies light
  On *Cassilis Downans* dance,
Or owre the lays, in splendid blaze,
  On sprightly coursers prance;
Or for *Colean*, the rout is taen,
  Beneath the moon's pale beams;
There, up the *Cove*, to stray an' rove
  Amang the rocks and streams
        To sport that night;

Amang the bonie, winding banks,
  Where *Doon* rins, wimplin, clear,
Where BRUCE ance rul'd the martial ranks,
  An' shook his *Carrick* spear,
Some merry, friendly, countra folks,
  Together did convene,
To *burn* their nits, an' pou their stocks,
  An' haud their *Halloween*
          Fu' blythe that night.

The lasses feat, an' cleanly neat,
  Mair braw than when they're fine ;
Their faces blythe, fu' sweetly kythe,
  Hearts leal, an' warm, an' kin :
The lads sae trig, wi' wooer-babs,
  Weel knotted on their garten,
Some unco blate, an' some wi' gabs,
  Gar lasses' hearts gang startin
          Whyles fast at night.

Then, first an' foremost, thro' the kail,
  Their *stocks* maun a' be sought ance :
They steek their een, an' grape an' wale,
  For muckle anes, an' straught anes.
Poor hav'rel *Will* fell aff the drift,
  An' wander'd thro' the *Bow-kail*,

An' pou't, for want o' better shift,
  A *runt* was like a sow-tail,
        Sae bow't that night.

Then, straught or crooked, yird or nane,
  They roar an' cry a' throw'ther;
The vera *wee-things*, toddlin, rin,
  Wi' stocks out-owre their shouther;
An' gif the custocks sweet or sour,
  Wi' joctelegs they taste them;
Syne coziely, aboon the door,
  Wi' cannie care, they've plac'd them
        To lye that night.

The lasses staw frae 'mang them a'
  To pou their *stalks o' corn*;
But *Rab* slips out, an' jinks about,
  Behint the muckle thorn:
He grippet *Nelly* hard an' fast;
  Loud skirl'd a' the lasses;
But her *tap-pickle* maist was lost,
  When kiutlin i' the Fause-house
        Wi' him that night.

The auld Guidwife's weel-hoordet *nits*
  Are round an' round divided,
An' monie lads' and lasses' fates
  Are there that night decided:

Some kindle, couthie, side by side,
   An' *burn* thegither trimly;
Some start awa, wi' saucy pride,
   An' jump out-owre the chimlie
          Fu' high that night.

Jean slips in twa, wi' tentie e'e;
   Wha 'twas, she wadna tell;
But this is *Jock*, and this is *me*,
   She says in to hersel:
He bleez'd owre her, an' she owre him,
   As they wad never mair part;
Till fuff! he started up the lum,
   An' *Jean* had e'en a sair heart
          To see't that night.

Poor Willie, wi' his *bow-kail runt*,
   Was *brunt* wi' primsie *Mallie*,
An' Mary, nae doubt, took the drunt,
   To be compar'd to Willie:
Mall's nit lap out, wi' pridefu' fling,
   An' her ain fit it brunt it;
While Willie lap, an' swoor by *jing*,
   'Twas just the way he wanted
          To be that night.

Nell had the Fause-house in her min',
   She pits hersel an' Rob in;

In loving bleeze they sweetly join,
  Till white in ase they're sobbin :
Nell's heart was dancin at the view ;
  She whisper'd *Rob* to leuk for't :
Rob, stownlins, prie'd her bonnie mou,
  Fu' cozie in the neuk for't,
          Unseen that night.

But *Merran* sat behint their backs,
  Her thoughts on *Andrew Bell ;*
She lea'es them gashan at their cracks,
  An' slips out by hersel :
She thro' the yard the nearest taks,
  An' to the *kiln* she goes then,
An' darklins grapet for the bauks,
  And in the *blue-clue* throws then,
          Right fear't that night.

An' aye she *win't,* an' ay she swat,
  I wat she made nae jaukin ;
Till something held within the *pat,*
  Guid Lord ! but she was quaukin !
But whether 'twas the Deil himsel,
  Or whether 'twas a *bauk-en',*
Or whether it was *Andrew Bell,*
  She did na wait on talkin
          To spier that night.

Wee Jenny to her Graunie says,
  "Will ye go wi' me, Graunie?
I'll *eat the apple* at the *glass*,
  I gat frae uncle Johnie:"
She fuff't her pipe wi' sic a lunt,
  In wrath she was sae vap'rin,
She notic't na, an aizle brunt
  Her braw, new worset apron
        Out thro' that night.

"Ye little Skelpie-limmer's-face!
  I daur you try sic sportin,
As seek the *foul Thief* onie place,
  For him to spae your fortune?
Nae doubt but ye may get a *sight!*
  Great cause ye hae to fear it;
For monie a ane has gotten a fright,
  An' liv'd an' di'd deleeret,
        On sic a night.

"Ae Hairst afore the *Sherra-moor*,
  I mind't as weel's yestreen,
I was a gilpey then, I'm sure
  I was na past fyfteen:
The simmer had been cauld an' wat,
  An' Stuff was unco' green;

An' ay a rantan *Kirn* we gat,
   An' just on *Halloween*
      It fell that night.

"Our *Stibble-rig* was *Rab M'Graen*,
   A clever, sturdy fallow;
His Sin gat Eppie Sim wi' wean,
   That liv'd in Achmacalla;
He gat *hemp-seed*, I mind it weel,
   An' he made unco light o't;
But monie a day was *by himsel*,
   He was sae sairly frighted
      That vera night."

Then up gat fechtin *Jamie Fleck*,
   An' he swoor by his conscience,
That he could *saw hemp-seed* a peck;
   For it was a' but nonsense:
The auld guidman raught down the pock,
   An' out a handfu' gied him;
Syne bad him slip frae 'mang the folk,
   Sometime when nae ane see'd him,
      An' try't that night.

He marches thro' amang the stacks,
   Tho' he was something sturtan;
The *graip* he for a *harrow* taks,
   An' haurls at his curpan:

An' ev'ry now an' then, he says,
    "Hemp-seed, I saw thee,
An' her that is to be my lass,
    Come after me an' draw thee
            As fast this night."

He whistl'd up *lord Lenox' march*,
    To keep his courage cheary;
Altho' his hair began to arch,
    He was sae fley'd an' eerie:
Till presently he hears a squeak,
    An' then a grane an' gruntle;
He by his shouther gae a keek,
    An' tumbl'd wi' a wintle
            Out owre that night.

He roar'd a horrid murder-shout,
    In dreadfu' desperation!
An' young an' auld come rinnan out,
    An' hear the sad narration:
He swoor 'twas hilchan *Jean M'Craw*,
    Or crouchie *Merran Humphie*,
Till stop! she trotted thro' them a';
    An' wha was it but *Grumphie*
            Asteer that night!

Meg fain wad to the Barn gaen
    To *winn three wechts o' naething;*

But for to meet the Deil her lane,
  She pat but little faith in :
She gies the Herd a pickle nits,
  And twa red-cheeket apples,
To watch, while for the Barn she sets,
  In hopes to see *Tam Kipples*
            That vera night.

She turns the key, wi' cannie thraw,
  An' owre the threshold ventures ;
But first on *Sawnie* gies a ca',
  Syne bauldly in she enters ;
A *ratton* rattl'd up the wa',
  An' she cry'd, Lord preserve her !
An' ran thro' midden-hole, an' a',
  An' pray'd wi' zeal an' fervour,
            Fu' fast that night.

They hoy't out Will, wi' sair advice ;
  They hecht him some fine braw ane ;
It chanc'd the *Stack* he *faddom't thrice*
  Was timmer-propt for thrawin :
He taks a swirlie, auld *moss-oak*,
  For some black, grousome *Carlin ;*
An' loot a winze, an' drew a stroke,
  Till skin in blypes cam haurlin
            Aff's nieves that night.

A wanton widow *Leezie* was,
    As cantie as a kittlen;
But Och! that night, amang the shaws,
    She gat a fearfu' settlin!
She thro' the whins, an' by the cairn,
    An' owre the hill gaed scrievin,
Whare *three lairds' lands met at a burn*,
    To dip her *left sark-sleeve* in,
             Was bent that night.

Whyles owre a linn the burnie plays,
    As thro' the glen it wimpl't;
Whyles round a rocky scar it strays;
    Whyles in a wiel it dimpl't;
Whyles glitter'd to the nightly rays,
    Wi' bickering, dancin dazzle;
Whyles cocket underneath the braes,
    Below the spreading hazle,
             Unseen that night.

Amang the brachens on the brae,
    Between her an' the moon,
The Diel, or else an outler Quey,
    Gat up an' gae a croon:
Poor *Leezie's* heart maist lap the hool;
    Near lav'rock-height she jumpet,

But mist a fit, an' in the *pool*
  Out owre the lugs she plumpet,
        Wi' a plunge that night.

In order, on the clean hearth-stane,
  The *Luggies* three are ranged;
And ev'ry time great care is ta'en,
  To see them duely changed:
Auld uncle *John*, wha *wedlock's joys*
  Sin' *Mar's-year* did desire,
Because he gat the toom dish thrice,
  He heav'd them on the fire
        In wrath that night.

Wi' merry sangs, and friendly cracks,
  I wat they did na weary;
And unco tales, an' funnie jokes,
  Their sports were cheap and cheary;
Till *butter'd So'ns*, wi' fragrant lunt,
  Set a' their gabs asteerin;
Syne, wi' a social glass o' strunt,
  They parted aff careerin
        Fu' blythe that night.

THE JOLLY BEGGARS.

A CANTATA.

RECITATIVO.

WHEN lyart leaves bestrow the yird,
    Or wavering like the Bauckie bird,
Bedim cauld Boreas' blast;
When hailstanes drive wi' bitter skyte,
And infant frosts begin to bite,
    In hoary cranreuch drest;
Ae night at e'en a merry core
    O' randie, gangrel bodies,
In Poosie-Nansie's held the splore,
    To drink their orra duddies:
      Wi' quaffing and laughing,
        They ranted and they sang;
      Wi' jumping and thumping,
        The verra girdle rang.

First, niest the fire, in auld red rags,
Ane sat; weel brac'd wi' mealy bags,
    And knapsack a' in order;

His doxy lay within his arm,
Wi' usquebae an' blankets warm,
 She blinket on her sodger:
An' aye he gies the tozie drab
 The tither skelpin' kiss,
While she held up her greedy gab,
 Just like an aumos dish.
  Ilk smack still, did crack still,
   Just like a cadger's whip,
  Then staggering and swaggering,
   He roar'd this ditty up—

AIR.

Tune—"*Soldier's Joy.*"

I am a son of Mars who have been in many wars,
And show my cuts and scars wherever I come;
This here was for a wench, and that other in a trench,
When welcoming the French at the sound of the drum.
            Lal de daudle, etc.

My 'prentiship I past where my leader breath'd his last,
When the bloody die was cast on the heights of Abram;
I serv'd out my trade when the gallant game was play'd,
And the Moro low was laid at the sound of the drum.
            Lal de daudle, etc.

I lastly was with Curtis, among the floating batt'ries,
And there I left for witness an arm and a limb:
Yet let my country need me, with Elliot to head me,
I'd clatter on my stumps at the sound of a drum.

       Lal de daudle, etc.

And now, tho' I must beg with a wooden arm and leg,
And many a tatter'd rag hanging over my bum,
I'm as happy with my wallet, my bottle and my callet,
As when I us'd in scarlet to follow a drum.

       Lal de daudle, etc.

What tho' with hoary locks, I must stand the winter shocks,
Beneath the woods and rocks oftentimes for a home;
When the tother bag I sell, and the tother bottle tell,
I could meet a troop of hell, at the sound of the drum.

RECITATIVO.

He ended; and the kebars sheuk,
 Aboon the chorus roar;
While frighted rattons backward leuk,
 And seek the benmost bore:
A fairy fiddler frae the neuk,
 He skirl'd out encore!
But up arose the martial chuck,
 And laid the loud uproar.

AIR.

Tune—"*Soldier Laddie.*"

I ONCE was a maid, tho' I cannot tell when,
And still my delight is in proper young men;
Some one of a troop of dragoons was my daddie,
No wonder I'm fond of a sodger laddie.
      Sing, Lal de lal, etc.

The first of my loves was a swaggering blade,
To rattle the thundering drum was his trade;
His leg was so tight, and his cheek was so ruddy,
Transported I was with my sodger laddie.
      Sing, Lal de lal, etc.

But the godly old chaplain left him in the lurch,
So the sword I forsook for the sake of the church;
He ventur'd the *soul*, I risked the *body*,
'Twas then I prov'd false to my sodger laddie.
      Sing, Lal de lal, etc.

Full soon I grew sick of my sanctified sot,
The regiment at large for a husband I got;
From the gilded spontoon to the fife I was ready,
I asked no more but a sodger laddie.
      Sing, Lal de lal, etc.

But the peace it reduc'd me to beg in despair,
Till I met my old boy at a Cunningham fair;
His *rags regimental* they flutter'd so gaudy,
My heart it rejoic'd at my sodger laddie.

      Sing, Lal de lal, etc.

And now I have liv'd—I know not how long,
And still I can join in a cup or a song;
But whilst with both hands I can hold the glass steady,
Here's to thee, my hero, my sodger laddie.

      Sing, Lal de lal, etc.

RECITATIVO.

Then niest outspak a raucle carlin,
Wha kent fu' weel to cleek the sterling,
For mony a pursie she had hooked,
And had in mony a wel been ducked;
Her dove had been a Highland laddie,
But weary fa' the waefu' woodie!
Wi' sighs and sabs, she thus began
To wail her braw John Highlandman.

AIR.

TUNE—"*O an' ye were dead, Guidman.*"

I.

A HIGHLAND lad my love was born,
The Lalland laws he held in scorn:

But he still was faithfu' to his clan,
My gallant, braw John Highlandman.

CHORUS.

Sing, hey my braw John Highlandman!
Sing, ho my braw John Highlandman!
There's not a lad in a' the lan'
    Was match for my John Highlandman.

II.

With his philibeg an' tartan plaid,
And gude claymore down by his side,
The ladies' hearts he did trepan,
My gallant, braw John Highlandman
          Sing, hey, etc.

III.

We ranged a' from Tweed to Spey,
And liv'd like lords and ladies gay;
For a Lalland face he feared nane,
My gallant, braw John Highlandman.
          Sing, hey, etc.

IV.

They banish'd him beyond the sea,
But ere the bud was on the tree,
Adown my checks the pearls ran,
Embracing my John Highlandman.
          Sing, hey, etc.

V.

But, oh! they catch'd him at the last,
And bound him in a dungeon fast;
My curse upon them every one,
They've hang'd my braw John Highlandman.
    Sing, hey, etc.

VI.

And now a widow, I must mourn
The pleasures that will ne'er return;
No comfort but a hearty can,
When I think on John Highlandman.
    Sing, hey, etc.

RECITATIVO.

A pigmy scraper wi' his fiddle,
Wha us'd at trysts and fairs to driddle,
Her strappan limb and gausy middle
    He reach'd nae higher,
Had hol'd his heartie like a riddle,
    And blawn't on fire.

Wi' hand on haunch, an' upward e'e,
He croon'd his gamut, one, two, three,
Then in an Arioso key,
    The wee Apollo
Set aff wi' *Allegretto* glee,
    His giga solo.

AIR.

Tune—"*Whistle owre the lave o't.*"

Let me ryke up to dight that tear,
An' go wi' me to be my dear,
An' then your every care and fear
   May whistle owre the lave o't.

CHORUS.

I am a fiddler to my trade,
And a' the tunes that e'er I play'd,
The sweetest still to wife or maid,
   Was whistle owre the lave o't.

At kirns an' weddings we'se be there,
And O! sae nicely's we will fare;
We'll bouse about till Daddie Care
   Sing, whistle owre the lave o't.
               I am, etc.

Sae merrily's the banes we'll pyke,
And sun oursells about the dyke,
And at our leisure when ye like,
   We'll whistle owre the lave o't.
               I am, etc.

But bless me wi' your heav'n o' charms,
And while I kittle hair on thairms,

> *Hunger*, *cauld*, and a' sic harms,
> May whistle owre the lave o't.
>
> I am, etc.

RECITATIVO.

> Her charms had struck a sturdy Caird,
> As well as poor Gutscraper;
> He taks the fiddler by the beard,
> And draws a roosty rapier—
> He swoor by a' was swearing worth,
> To speet him like a pliver,
> Unless he wou'd from that time forth
> Relinquish her for ever.
>
> Wi' ghastly ee, poor tweedle-dee
> Upon his hunkers bended,
> And pray'd for grace wi' ruefu' face,
> An' so the quarrel ended.
> But tho' his little heart did grieve
> When round the tinkler prest her,
> He feign'd to snirtle in his sleeve,
> When thus the Caird address'd her.

AIR.

Tune—"*Clout the Cauldron.*"

> My bonnie lass I work in brass,
> A tinker is my station;

I've travell'd round all Christian ground
    In this my occupation.
I've ta'en the gold, I've been enroll'd
    In many a noble squadron;
But vain they search'd, when off I march'd
    To go an clout the caudron.
          I've ta'en the gold, etc.

Despise that shrimp, that wither'd imp,
    Wi' a' his noise and caprin',
An' tak a share wi' those that bear
    The *budget* an' the *apron;*
And by that stowp! my faith and houpe,
    And by that dear Keilbaigie,
If e'er ye want, or meet wi' scant,
    May I ne'er weet my craigie.
          And by that stowp, etc.

RECITATIVO.

The Caird prevail'd—th' unblushing fair
    In his embraces sunk,
Partly wi' love o'ercome sae sair,
    An' partly she was drunk.
Sir Violinos with an air,
    That show'd a man of spunk,

Wish'd *unison* between the pair,
   And made the bottle clunk
          To their health that night.

But hurchin Cupid shot a shaft
   That play'd a dame a shavie,
The fiddler rak'd her fore and aft,
   Behint the chicken cavie.
Her lord, a wight o' Homer's craft,
   Tho' limping wi' the spavie,
He hirpl'd up, and lap like daft,
   And shor'd them Dainty Davie.
          O boot that night.

He was a care-defying blade
   As ever Bacchus listed,
Tho' Fortune sair upon him laid,
   His heart she ever miss'd it.
He had nae wish but—to be glad,
   Nor want but—when he thristed;
He hated nought but—to be sad,
   And thus the muse suggested
          His sang that night.

AIR.

TUNE—"*For a' that, and a' that.*"

I AM a bard of no regard
   Wi' gentle folks, an' a' that;

But *Homer-like*, the glowran byke,
Frae town to town I draw that.

CHORUS.

For a' that, and a' that,
   And twice as muckle 's a' that;
I've lost but ane, I've twa behin',
   I've *wife eneugh* for a' that.

I never drank the Muses' stank,
   Castalia's burn, an' a' that;
But there it streams, and richly reams,
   My *Helicon* I ca' that.
                For a' that, etc.

Great love I bear to a' the fair,
   Their humble slave, an' a' that;
But lordly will, I hold it still
   A mortal sin to thraw that.
                For a' that, etc.

In raptures sweet, this hour we meet,
   Wi' mutual love, an' a' that;
But for how lang the *flie my stang*,
   Let *inclina'ion* law that.
                For a' that, etc.

Their tricks and craft have put me daft,
    They've ta'en me in, and a' that;
But clear your decks, and here's the *sex!*
    I like the jads for a' that.

   For a' that, and a' that,
      And twice as muckle 's a' that;
   My *dearest bluid*, to do them guid,
      They're welcome till't for a' that.

RECITATIVO.

So sung the bard—and Nansie's wa's
Shook with a thunder of applause,
    Re-echo'd from each mouth;
They toom'd their pocks, an' pawn'd their duds,
They scarcely left to cooer their fuds,
    To quench their lowan drouth.

Then owre again, the jovial thrang
    The poet did request
To lowse his pack an' wale a sang,
    A ballad o' the best;
He, rising, rejoicing,
    Between his twa *Deborahs,*
Looks round him, an' found them
    Impatient for the chorus.

AIR.

TUNE—"*Jolly Mortals fill your Glasses.*"

I.

SEE ! the smoking bowl before us,
    Mark our jovial ragged ring !
Round and round take up the chorus,
    And in raptures let us sing.

CHORUS.

A fig for those by law protected !
    Liberty's a glorious feast !
Courts for cowards were erected,
    Churches built to please the priest.

II.

What is title ? what is treasure ?
    What is reputation's care ?
If we lead a life of pleasure,
    'Tis no matter *how* or *where !*
            A fig, etc.

III.

With the ready trick and fable,
    Round we wander all the day ;
And at night, in barn or stable,
    Hug our doxies on the hay.
            A fig, etc.

IV.

Does the train-attended *carriage*
  Through the country lighter rove ?
Does the sober bed of marriage
  Witness brighter scenes of love ?
      A fig, etc.

V.

Life is all a *variorum*,
  We regard not how it goes ;
Let them cant about *decorum*
  Who have characters to lose.
      A fig, etc.

VI.

Here's to budgets, bags, and wallets !
  Here's to all the wandering train !
Here's our ragged *brats* and *callets !*
  One and all cry out, Amen !

A fig for those by law protected !
  Liberty's a glorious feast !
Courts for cowards were erected,
  Churches built to please the priest.

THE AULD FARMER'S NEW-YEAR MORNING SALUTATION TO HIS AULD MARE, MAGGIE,

ON GIVING HER THE ACCUSTOMED RIPP OF CORN TO HANSEL IN THE NEW YEAR.

A *GUID New-Year* I wish thee Maggie!
Hae, there's a ripp to thy auld baggie:
Tho' thou's howe-backet, now, an' knaggie,
  I've seen the day,
Thou could hae gane like ony staggie
  Out-owre the lay.

Tho' now thou's dowie, stiff an' crazy,
An' thy auld hide's as white's a daisie,
I've seen thee dappl't, sleek an' glaizie,
  A bonie gray:
He should been tight that daur't to *raize* thee,
  Ance in a day.

Thou ance was i' the foremost rank,
A *filly* buirdly, steeve, an' swank,
An' set weel down a shapely shank,
  As e'er tread yird;
An' could hae flown out-owre a stank,
  Like onie bird.

It's now some nine-an'-twenty year,
Sin' thou was my *Guid father's Meere;*
He gied me thee, o' tocher clear,
   An' fifty mark;
Tho' it was sma' 'twas *weel-won* gear,
   An' thou was stark.

When first I gaed to woo my *Jenny*,
Ye then was trottan wi' your minnie:
Tho' ye was trickie, slee, an' funnie,
   Ye ne'er was donsie;
But hamely, tawie, quiet, an' cannie,
   An' unco sonsie.

That *day*, ye pranc'd wi' muckle pride,
When ye bure hame my bonie *Bride;*
An' sweet an' gracefu' she did ride,
   Wi' maiden air!
KYLE-STEWART I could bragged wide,
   For sic a pair.

Tho' now ye dow but hoyte and hoble,
An' wintle like a saumont-coble,
That day ye was a jinker noble
   For heels an' win'!
An' ran them till they a' did wauble,
   Far, far behin'.

When thou an' I were young and skeigh,
An' *Stable-meals* at fairs were driegh,
How thou wad prance, an' snore, an' skreigh,
   An' tak the road !
Town's-bodies ran, and stood abeigh,
   An' ca't thee mad.

When thou was corn't, an' I was mellow,
We took the road ay like a Swallow:
At *Brooses* thou had ne'er a fellow,
   For pith an' speed ;
But ev'ry tail thou pay't them hollow,
   Whare'er thou gaed.

The sma', droop-rumpl't, hunter cattle,
Might aiblins waur't thee for a brattle ;
But *sax Scotch mile* thou try't their mettle,
   An' gart them whaizle :
Nae whip nor spur, but just a wattle
   O' saugh or hazle.

Thou was a noble *Fittie-lan'*,
As e'er in tug or tow was drawn !
Aft thee an' I, in aught hours gaun,
   On guid March-weather,
Hae turn'd *sax rood* beside our han',
   For days thegither.

Thou never braing't, an' fetch't, an' flisket,
But thy *auld tail* thou wad hae whisket,
An' spread abreed thy weel-fill'd *brisket*,
   Wi' pith an' pow'r,
Till sprittie knowes wad rair't and risket,
   An' slypet owre.

When frosts lay lang, an' snaws were deep,
An' threaten'd *labor* back to keep,
I gied thy *cog* a wee-bit heap
   Aboon the timmer;
ken'd my *Maggie* wad na sleep
   For that, or Simmer.

In *cart* or *car* thou never reestet;
The steyest brae thou wad hae fac't it;
Thou never lap, an' sten't and breastet,
   Then stood to blaw;
But just thy step a wee thing hastit,
   Thou snoov't awa.

My Pleugh is now thy *bairn-time* a' :
Four gallant brutes as e'er did draw ;
Forbye sax mae, I've sell't awa,
   That thou hast nurst :
They drew me thretteen pund an' twa
   The vera warst.

Monie a sair daurk we twa hae wrought,
An' wi' the weary warl' fought !
An' monie an *anxious day*, I thought
   We wad be beat !
Yet here to *crazy Age* we're brought,
   Wi' something yet.

And think na, my auld, trusty *Servan'*,
That now perhaps thou's less deservin,
An' thy *auld days* may end in starvin,
   For my last fou,
A heapet Stimpart, I'll reserve ane
   Laid by for you.

We've worn to crazy years thegither ;
We'll toyte about wi' ane anither ;
Wi' tentie care I'll flit thy tether
   To some hain'd rig,
Whare ye may nobly rax your leather,
   Wi' sma' fatigue.

THE COTTER'S SATURDAY NIGHT.

INSCRIBED TO ROBERT AIKEN, ESQ. OF AYR.

Let not Ambition mock their useful toil,
Their homely joys, and destiny obscure;
Nor Grandeur hear, with a disdainful smile,
The short and simple annals of the Poor.
                                       GRAY.

MY lov'd, my honour'd, much respected friend!
   No mercenary Bard his homage pays:
With honest pride, I scorn each selfish end;
   My dearest meed, a friend's esteem and praise:
To you I sing, in simple Scottish lays,
   The *lowly train* in life's sequester'd scene;
The native feelings strong, the guileless ways;
   What Aiken in a *Cottage* would have been;
Ah! tho' his worth unknown, far happier there I ween.

November chill blaws loud wi' angry sugh;
   The short'ning winter-day is near a close;
The miry beasts retreating frae the pleugh;
   The black'ning trains o' craws to their repose:
The toil-worn COTTER frae his labor goes,
   This night his weekly moil is at an end,

Collects his *spades*, his *mattocks*, and his *hoes*,
　Hoping the *morn* in ease and rest to spend,
And weary, o'er the moor, his course does hameward bend.

At length his lonely *Cot* appears in view,
　Beneath the shelter of an agèd tree ;
The expectant *wee-things*, toddlan, stacher through
　To meet their *Dad*, wi' flichterin noise an' glee.
His wee bit ingle, blinkan bonilie,
　His clean hearth-stane, his thrifty *Wifie's* smile,
The *lisping infant*, prattling on his knee,
　Does a' his weary kiaugh and care beguile,
An' makes him quite forget his labour an' his toil.

Belyve, the *elder bairns* come drapping in,
　At *Service* out, amang the Farmers roun' ;
Some ca' the pleugh, some herd, some tentie rin
　A cannie errand to a neebor town :
Their eldest hope, their *Jenny*, woman-grown,
　In youthfu' bloom, Love sparkling in her e'e,
Comes hame, perhaps, to shew a braw new gown,
　Or deposite her sair-won penny-fee,
To help her *Parents dear*, if they in hardship be.

With joy unfeign'd, *brothers* and *sisters* meet,
　An' each for other's weelfare kindly spiers :
The social hours, swift-wing'd, unnotic'd fleet ;
　Each tells the uncos that he sees or hears ;

The Parents partial eye their hopeful years ;
  Anticipation forward points the view.
The *Mother*, wi' her needle an' her sheers,
  Gars auld claies look amaist as weel's the new;
The *Father* mixes a' wi' admonition due.

Their Master's an' their Mistress's command,
  The *younkers* a' are warnèd to obey ;
An' mind their labours wi' an eydent hand,
  An' ne'er, tho' out o' sight, to jauk or play :
An' O ! be sure to fear the LORD alway,
  " An' mind your *duty*, duely, morn an' night !
Lest in temptation's path ye gang astray,
  Implore his *counsel* and assisting *might :*
They never sought in vain that sought the LORD aright ! "

But hark ! a rap comes gently to the door,
  Jenny, wha kens the meaning o' the same,
Tells how a neebor lad cam o'er the moor,
  To do some errands, and convoy her hame.
The wily Mother sees the *conscious flame*
  Sparkle in Jenny's e'e, and flush her cheek ;
Wi' heart-struck, anxious care, inquires his name,
  While Jenny hafflins is afraid to speak ;
Weel pleas'd the Mother hears, it's nae wild, worthless *Rake*.

Wi' kindly welcome, *Jenny* brings him ben ;
  A *strappan youth ;* he takes the Mother's eye ;

Blythe Jenny sees the *visit's* no ill ta'en;
 The Father cracks of horses, pleughs, and kye.
The *Youngster's* artless heart o'erflows wi' joy,
 But blate and laithfu', scarce can weel behave;
The Mother, wi' a woman's wiles, can spy
 What makes the *youth* sae bashfu' an' sae grave;
Weel-pleas'd to think her *bairn's* respected like the lave.

O happy love! where love like this is found!
 O heart-felt raptures! bliss beyond compare!
I've paced much this weary, *mortal round*,
 And sage EXPERIENCE bids me this declare—
" If Heaven a draught of heavenly pleasure spare,
 One *cordial* in this melancholy *Vale*,
'Tis when a youthful, loving, *modest* Pair,
 In other's arms breathe out the tender tale,
Beneath the milk-white thorn that scents the ev'ning gale."

Is there, in human form, that bears a heart—
 A Wretch! a Villain! lost to love and truth!
That can, with studied, sly, ensnaring art,
 Betray sweet Jenny's unsuspecting youth?
Curse on his perjur'd arts! dissembling smooth!
 Are Honor, Virtue, Conscience, all exil'd?
Is there no Pity, no relenting Ruth,
 Points to the Parents fondling o'er their Child?
Then paints the *ruin'd Maid*, and *their* distraction wild!

But now the Supper crowns their simple board,
  The healsome porritch, chief o' SCOTIA's food:
The soupe their *only Hawkie* does afford,
  That 'yont the hallan snugly chows her cood;
The *Dame* brings forth in complimental mood,
  To grace the lad, her weel-hain'd kebbuck, fell.
An' aft he's prest, an' aft he ca's it guid;
  The frugal *Wifie*, garrulous, will tell,
How 'twas a towmond auld, sin' Lint was i' the bell.

The chearfu' Supper done, wi' serious face,
  They, round the ingle, form a circle wide;
The Sire turns o'er, wi' patriarchal grace,
  The big *ha'-Bible*, ance his Father's pride:
His bonnet rev'rently is laid aside,
  His *lyart haffets* wearing thin an' bare;
Those strains that once did sweet in ZION glide,
  He wales a portion with judicious care,
"And let us worship GOD!" he says, with solemn air.

They chant their artless notes in simple guise;
  They tune their *hearts*, by far the noblest aim:
Perhaps *Dundee's* wild warbling measures rise,
  Or plaintive *Martyrs*, worthy of the name;
Or noble *Elgin* beets the heav'nward flame,
  The sweetest far of SCOTIA's holy lays:

Compar'd with these, *Italian trills* are tame;
   The tickl'd ears no heartfelt raptures raise;
Nae unison hae they with our CREATOR's praise.

The priest-like Father reads the sacred page,
   How *Abram* was the Friend of GOD on high;
Or, Moses bade eternal warfare wage,
   With *Amalek's* ungracious progeny;
Or how the *royal Bard* did groaning lie
   Beneath the stroke of Heaven's avenging ire;
Or *Job's* pathetic plaint, and wailing cry;
   Or rapt *Isaiah's* wild, seraphic fire;
Or other *Holy Seers* that tune the *sacred lyre*.

Perhaps the *Christian Volume* is the theme,
   How *guiltless blood* for *guilty man* was shed;
How HE, who bore in heaven the second name,
   Had not on Earth whereon to lay His head;
How His first *followers* and *servants* sped;
   The *Precepts* sage they wrote to many a land:
How *he*, who lone in *Patmos* banished,
   Saw in the sun a mighty angel stand;
And heard great *Bab'lon's* doom pronounc'd by Heaven's command.

Then kneeling down to HEAVEN'S ETERNAL KING,
   The *Saint*, the *Father*, and the *Husband* prays:

Hope ' springs exulting on triumphant wing,'
    That *thus* they all shall meet in future days:
There ever bask in *uncreated rays*,
    No more to sigh, or shed the bitter tear,
Together hymning their CREATOR's praise,
    In *such society*, yet still more dear;
While circling Time moves round in an eternal sphere.

Compar'd with *this*, how poor Religion's pride,
    In all the pomp of *method*, and of *art*,
When men display to congregations wide
    Devotion's ev'ry grace, except the heart!
The POWER, incens'd, the Pageant will desert,
    The pompous strain, the sacerdotal stole;
But haply, in some *Cottage* far apart,
    May hear, well pleas'd the language of the *Soul;*
And in his *Book of Life* the inmates poor enrol.

Then homeward all take off their sev'ral way;
    The youngling *Cottagers* retire to rest:
The *Parent-pair* their *secret homage* pay,
    And proffer up to Heaven the warm request,
That HE who stills the *raven's* clam'rous nest,
    And decks the *lily* fair in flow'ry pride,
Would, in the way *His Wisdom* sees the best,
    For *them* and for their *little ones* provide;
But chiefly, in their hearts with *Grace divine* preside.

From scenes like these old SCOTIA's grandeur springs,
    That makes her loved at home, rever'd abroad:
Princes and lords are but the breath of kings,
    "An honest man's the noble work of GOD:"
And *certes*, in fair Virtue's heavenly road,
    The *Cottage* leaves the *Palace* far behind;
What is a lordling's pomp? a cumbrous load,
    Disguising oft the *wretch* of human kind,
Studied in arts of Hell, in wickedness refined!

O SCOTIA! my dear, my native soil!
    For whom my warmest wish to heaven is sent!
Long may thy hardy sons of *rustic toil*
    Be blest with health, and peace, and sweet content!
And O may Heaven their simple lives prevent
    From *Luxury's* contagion, weak and vile;
Then, howe'er *crowns* and *coronets* be rent,
    A *virtuous Populace* may rise the while,
And stand a wall of fire around their much-loved ISLE.

O THOU! who pour'd the *patriotic tide*
    That stream'd thro' great, unhappy Wallace' heart;
Who dared to, nobly, stem tyrannic pride,
    Or nobly die, the second glorious part:

(The patriot's GOD, peculiarly thou art,
　　His *friend, inspirer, guardian,* and *reward!*)
O never, never, SCOTIA'S realm desert,
　　But still the *Patriot*, and the *Patriot-Bard*,
In bright succession raise, her *Ornament* and *Guard!*

A PRAYER, IN THE PROSPECT OF DEATH.

WHY am I loth to leave this earthly scene?
　　Have I so found it full of pleasing charms?
Some drops of joy with draughts of ill between,
　　Some gleams of sunshine 'mid renewing storms:
Is it departing pangs my soul alarms?
　　Or Death's unlovely, dreary, dark abode?
For guilt, for guilt, my terrors are in arms;
　　I tremble to approach an angry GOD,
And justly smart beneath his sin-avenging rod.

Fain would I say, "Forgive my foul offence!"
　　Fain promise never more to disobey;
But, should my Author health again dispense,
　　Again I might desert fair Virtue's way;
Again in Folly's path might go astray;
　　Again exalt the brute and sink the man;

Then how should I for Heavenly Mercy pray,
  Who act so counter Heavenly Mercy's plan?
Who sin so oft have mourn'd, yet to temptation ran?

O Thou, Great Governor of all below!
  If I may dare a lifted eye to Thee,
Thy nod can make the tempest cease to blow,
  And still the tumult of the raging sea:
With that controuling pow'r assist ev'n me,
  Those headlong, furious passions to confine,
For all unfit I feel my powers be,
  To rule their torrent in th' allowed line;
O, aid me with Thy help, *Omnipotence Divine!*

A PRAYER, UNDER THE PRESSURE OF VIOLENT ANGUISH.

O THOU great Being! what Thou art,
  Surpasses me to know:
Yet sure I am, that known to Thee
  Are all Thy works below.

Thy creature here before Thee stands,
  All wretched and distrest;
Yet sure those ills that wring my soul
  Obey Thy high behest.

Sure, Thou, Almighty, canst not act
   From cruelty or wrath!
O, free my weary eyes from tears,
   Or close them fast in death!

But if I must afflicted be,
   To suit some wise design;
Then, man my soul with firm resolves
   To bear and not repine!

TO A MOUNTAIN DAISY,

ON TURNING ONE DOWN WITH THE PLOUGH, IN APRIL, 1786.

WEE, modest, crimson-tipped flow'r,
   Thou's met me in an evil hour;
For I maun crush amang the stoure
         Thy slender stem.
To spare thee now is past my pow'r,
         Thou bonie gem.

Alas! it's no thy neebor sweet,
The bonie *Lark*, companion meet!

Bending thee 'mang the dewy weet !
           Wi' spreckl'd breast,
When upward-springing, blythe, to greet
           The purpling East.

Cauld blew the bitter-biting *North*
Upon thy early, humble birth ;
Yet chearfully thou glinted forth
           Amid the storm,
Scarce rear'd above the parent-earth
           Thy tender form.

The flaunting *flow'rs* our Gardens yield,
High shelt'ring woods and wa's maun shield,
But thou, beneath the random bield
           O' clod or stane,
Adorns the histie *stibble-field*,
           Unseen, alane.

There, in thy scanty mantle clad,
Thy snawie bosom sun-ward spread,
Thou lifts thy unassuming head
           In humble guise ;
But now the *share* uptears thy bed,
           And low thou lies !

Such is the fate of artless Maid,
Sweet *flow'ret* of the rural shade !
By Love's simplicity betray'd,
    And guileless trust,
Till she, like thee, all soil'd, is laid
    Low i' the dust.

Such is the fate of simple Bard,
On Life's rough ocean luckless starr'd !
Unskilful he to note the card
    Of *prudent Lore*,
Till billows rage, and gales blow hard,
    And whelm him o'er !

Such fate to *suffering worth* is giv'n,
Who long with wants and woes has striv'n,
By human pride or cunning driv'n
    To Mis'ry's brink,
Till wrench'd of ev'ry stay but HEAV'N,
    He, ruin'd, sink !

Ev'n thou who mourn'st the *Daisy's* fate,
That fate is thine—no distant date ;
Stern Ruin's *ploughshare* drives, elate,
    Full on thy bloom,
Till crush'd beneath the *furrow's* weight,
    Shall be thy doom !

EPISTLE TO A YOUNG FRIEND.

MAY, 1786.

I LANG hae thought, my youthfu' friend,
    A Something to have sent you,
Tho' it should serve nae ither end
    Than just a kind memento;
But how the subject theme may gang,
    Let time and chance determine;
Perhaps, it may turn out a Sang,
    Perhaps, turn out a Sermon.

Ye'll try the world soon my lad,
    And ANDREW dear, believe me,
Ye'll find mankind an unco squad,
    And muckle they may grieve ye:
For care and trouble set your thought,
    Ev'n when your end's attained;
And a' your views may come to nought,
    Where ev'ry nerve is strained.

I'll no say men are villains a';
    The real, harden'd wicked,
Wha hae nae check but *human law*,
    Are to a few restricked:

But Och, mankind are unco weak,
    An' little to be trusted;
If *Self* the wavering balance shake,
    It's rarely right adjusted!

Yet they wha fa' in Fortune's strife,
    Their fate we should na censure,
For still th' important end of life
    They equally may answer;
A man may hae an *honest heart*,
    Tho' Poortith hourly stare him;
A man may tak a neebor's part,
    Yet hae nae *cash* to spare him.

Aye free, aff han', your story tell,
    When wi' a bosom crony;
But still keep something to yoursel
    Ye scarcely tell to ony.
Conceal yoursel as weel's ye can
    Frae critical dissection;
But keek thro' ev'ry other man,
    Wi' sharpen'd, sly inspection.

The *sacred lowe* o' weel-placed love,
    Luxuriantly indulge it;
But never tempt th' *illicit rove*,
    Tho' naething should divulge it;

I wave the quantum o' the sin,
    The hazard o' concealing,
But Och ! it hardens *a' within*,
    And petrifies the feeling !

To catch Dame Fortune's golden smile,
    Assiduous wait upon her ;
And gather gear by ev'ry wile
    That's justify'd by Honor ;
Not for to hide it in a *hedge*,
    Nor for a *train-attendant ;*
But for the glorious privilege
    Of being *independent.*

The *fear o' hell's* a hangman's whip,
    To haud the wretch in order ;
But where ye feel your Honor grip,
    Let that aye be your border :
Its slightest touches, instant pause—
    Debar a' side pretences ;
And resolutely keep its laws,
    Uncaring consequences.

The great CREATOR to revere,
    Must sure become the *Creature ;*
But still the preaching cant forbear,
    And ev'n the rigid feature :

Yet ne'er with Wits profane to range,
  Be complaisance extended ;
An atheist-laugh's a poor exchange
  For *Deity offended!*

When ranting round in Pleasure's ring,
  Religion may be blinded ;
Or if she gie a *random-sting*,
  It may be little minded ;
But when on Life we're tempest-driv'n,
  A Conscience but a canker—
A correspondence fix'd wi' Heav'n
  Is sure a noble *anchor!*

Adieu, dear, amiable Youth !
  Your *heart* can ne'er be wanting !
May Prudence, Fortitude and Truth,
  Erect your brow undaunting !
In *ploughman phrase*, ' GOD send you speed,'
  Still daily to grow wiser ;
And may ye better reck the *rede*,
  Than ever did th' *Adviser!*

TO A HAGGIS.

FAIR fa' your honest, sonsie face,
    Great Chieftain o' the Puddin'-race !
Aboon them a' ye tak your place,
        Painch, tripe, or thairm :
Weel are ye wordy o' a *grace*
        As lang's my arm.

The groaning trencher there ye fill,
Your hurdies like a distant hill,
Your *pin* wad help to mend a mill
        In time o' need,
While thro' your pores the dews destil
        Like amber bead.

His knife see Rustic-labour dight,
An' cut you up wi' ready slight,
Trenching your gushing entrails bright
        Like onie ditch ;
And then, O what a glorious sight,
        Warm-reekin, rich !

Then, horn for horn they stretch an' strive,
Deil tak the hindmost, on they drive,
Till a' their weel-swall'd kytes belyve
      Are bent like drums;
Then auld Guidman, maist like to rive,
      Bethankit hums.

Is there that o'er his French *ragout*,
Or *olio* that wad staw a sow,
Or *fricassee* wad mak her spew
      Wi' perfect sconner,
Looks down wi' sneering, scornfu' view
      On sic a dinner?

Poor devil! see him owre his trash,
As feckless as a wither'd rash,
His spindle shank a guid whip-lash,
      His nieve a nit;
Thro' bloody flood or field to dash,
      O how unfit!

But mark the Rustic, *haggis-fed*,
The trembling earth resounds his tread,
Clap in his walie nieve a blade,
      He'll mak it whissle;
An' legs, an' arms, an' heads will sned,
      Like taps o' thrissle.

Ye Pow'rs wha mak mankind your care,
And dish them out their bill o' fare,
Auld Scotland wants nae skinking ware
  That jaups in luggies;
But, if ye wish her gratefu' pray'r,
  Gie her a *Haggis!*

TO W * * * S * * *

OCHILTREE

May, 1785.

I GAT your letter, winsome Willie;
Wi' gratefu' heart I thank you brawlie;
Tho' I maun say't, I wad be silly,
  An' unco vain,
Should I believe, my coaxin billie,
  Your flatterin strain.

But I'se believe ye kindly meant it,
I sud be laith to think ye hinted
Ironic satire, sidelins sklented
  On my poor Musie;
Tho' in sic phraisin terms ye've penn'd it,
  I scarce excuse ye.

My senses wad be in a creel,
Should I but dare a *hope* to speel,
Wi' *Allan*, or wi' *Gilbertfield*,
  The braes o' fame;
Or *Ferguson*, the writer-chiel,
  A deathless name.

(O Ferguson! thy glorious *parts*
Ill suited *law's* dry, musty arts!
My curse upon your whunstane hearts,
  Ye Enbrugh Gentry!
The tythe o' what ye waste at *cartes*
  Wad stow'd his pantry!)

Yet when a tale comes i' my head,
Or lasses gie my heart a screed,
As whiles they're like to be my dead,
  (O sad disease!)
I kittle up my *rustic reed*;
  It gies me ease.

Auld COILA, now, may fidge fu' fain,
She's gotten Bardies o' her ain,
Chiels wha their chanters winna hain,
  But tune their lays,
Till echoes a' resound again
  Her weel-sung praise.

Nae *Poet* thought her worth his while,
To set her name in measur'd style;
She lay like some unkend-of isle,
   Beside *New Holland*,
Or whare wild-meeting oceans *boil*
   Besouth *Magellan*.

Ramsay an' famous *Ferguson*
Gied *Forth* an' *Tay* a lift aboon;
Yarrow an' *Tweed*, to monie a tune,
   Owre Scotland rings.
While *Irwin, Lugar, Aire* an' *Doon*,
   Naebody sings.

Th' *Ilissus, Tiber, Thames*, an' *Seine*,
Glide sweet in monie a tunefu' line!
But *Willie*, set your fit to mine,
   An' cock your crest,
We'll gar our streams an' burnies shine
   Up wi' the best.

We'll sing auld COILA's plains an' fells,
Her moors red-brown wi' heather bells,
Her banks an' braes, her dens an' dells,
   Where glorious WALLACE
Aft bure the gree, as story tells,
   Frae Southron billies.

At WALLACE' name, what Scottish blood
But boils up in a spring-tide flood !
Oft have our fearless fathers strode
    By WALLACE' side,
Still pressing onward, red-wat-shod,
    Or glorious dy'd.

O, sweet are COILA'S haughs an' woods,
When lintwhites chant amang the buds,
And jinkin hares, in amorous whids,
    Their loves enjoy,
While thro' the braes the cushat croods
    Wi' wailfu' cry !

Ev'n winter bleak has charms to me
When winds rave thro' the naked tree ;
Or frosts on hills of *Ochiltree*
    Are hoary gray ;
Or blinding drifts wild-furious flee,
    Dark'ning the day !

O NATURE! a' thy shews an' forms
To feeling, pensive hearts hae charms !
Whether the Summer kindly warms,
    Wi' life an' light,
Or Winter howls, in gusty storms,
    The lang, dark night !

The *Muse*, na *Poet* ever fand her,
Till by himsel he learn'd to wander,
Adown some trottin burns meander,
   An' no think lang ;
O sweet, to stray an' pensive ponder
   A heart-felt sang !

The warly race may drudge an' drive,
Hog-shouther, jundie, stretch, an' strive,
Let me fair NATURE'S face descrive,
   And I, wi' pleasure,
Shall let the busy, grumbling hive
   Bum owre their treasure.

Fareweel, " my rhyme-composing brither"
We've been owre lang unkenn'd to ither :
Now let us lay our heads thegither,
   In love fraternal :
May *Envy* wallop in a tether,
   Black fiend, infernal !

While Highlandmen hate tolls an' taxes ;
While moorlan' herds like guid, fat braxies ;
While Terra firma, on her axis,
   Diurnal turns,
Count on a friend, in faith an' practice,
   In ROBERT BURNS.

POSTSCRIPT.

MY memory's no worth a preen;
    I had amaist forgotten clean,
Ye bad me write you what they mean
      By this *new-light*,[1]
'Bout which our *herds* sae aft have been
      Maist like to fight.

In days when mankind were but callans
At *Grammar*, *Logic*, an' sic talents,
They took nae pains their speech to balance,
      Or rules to gie,
But spak their thoughts in plain, braid lallans,
      Like you or me.

In thae auld times, they thought the *Moon*,
Just like a sark, or pair o' shoon,
Woor by degrees, till her last roon,
      Gaed past their viewin,
An' shortly after she was done,
      They gat a new ane.

---

[1] A cant term for those religious opinions, which Dr. Taylor, of Norwich defended so strenuously.

This past for certain, undisputed;
It ne'er cam i' their heads to doubt it,
Till chiels gat up an' wad confute it,
    An' ca'd it wrang;
An' muckle din there was about it,
    Baith loud an' lang.

Some *herds*, weel learn'd upo' the beuk,
Wad threap auld folk the thing misteuk;
For 'twas the *auld moon* turn'd a neuk,
    An' out o' sight,
An' backlins-comin, to the leuk,
    She grew mair bright.

This was deny'd, it was affirm'd;
The *herds* an' *hissels* were alarm'd:
The rev'rend gray-beards rav'd and storm'd,
    That beardless laddies
Should think they better were inform'd,
    Than their auld daddies.

Frae less to mair it gaed to sticks;
Frae words an' aiths to clours an' nicks;
An' monie a fallow gat his licks,
    Wi' hearty crunt;
An' some, to learn them for their tricks,
    Were hang'd an' brunt.

This game was play'd in monie lands,
An' *auld-light* caddies bure sic hands,
That, faith, the *youngsters* took the sands
    Wi' nimble shanks,
Till *Lairds* forbad, by strict commands,
    Sic bluidy pranks.

But *new-light herds* gat sic a cowe,
Folk thought them ruin'd stick-an-stowe,
Till now amaist on ev'ry *knowe*
    Ye'll find ane plac'd ;
An' some, their *New-light* fair avow,
    Just quite barefac'd.

Nae doubt the *auld-light flocks* are bleatan ;
Their zealous *herds* are vex'd an' sweatan ;
Mysel, I've even seen them greetan
    Wi' girnan spite,
To hear the *Moon* sae sadly lie'd on
    By word an' write.

But shortly they will cowe the louns !
Some *auld-light* herds in neebor towns
Are mind't, in things they ca' *balloons*,
    To tak a flight,
An' stay ae month amang the *Moons*,
    An' see them right.

Guid observation they will gie them;
An' when the *auld Moon's* gaun to lea'e them;
The hindmost *shaird*, they'll fetch it wi' them,
   Just i' their pouch,
An' when the new-light billies see them,
   I think they'll crouch!

Sae, ye observe that a' this clatter
Is naething but a "moonshine matter;"
But tho' dull-prose folk latin splatter
   In logic tulzie,
I hope we, *Bardies* ken some better
   Than mind sic brulzie.

EPISTLE TO JOHN RANKIN,

ENCLOSING SOME POEMS.

O ROUGH, rude, ready-witted Rankin,
 The wale o' cocks for fun an' drinkin!
There's monie godly folks are thinkin,
   Your *dreams* an' tricks
Will send you, Korah-like,[1] a-sinkin,
   Straught to auld Nick's.

---

[1] A certain humorous *dream* of his was then making a noise in the world.

Ye hae sae monie cracks an' cants,
And in your wicked, druken rants,
Ye mak a devil o' the *Saunts*,
  An' fill them fou;
And then their failings, flaws, an' wants,
  Are a' seen thro'.

Hypocrisy, in mercy spare it!
That *holy robe*, O dinna tear it!
Spare't for their sakes wha aften wear it,
  The lads in *black*;
But your curst wit, when it comes near it,
  Rives't aff their back.

Think, wicked Sinner, wha ye're skaithing,
It's just the *Blue-gown* badge an' claithing,
O' Saunts; tak that, ye lea'e them naething
  To ken them by,
Frae ony unregenerate Heathen
  Like you or I.

I've sent you here, some rhyming ware,
A' that I bargain'd for, an' mair;
Sae when ye hae an hour to spare,
  I will expect,
Yon *Sang*[1] ye'll sen't, wi' cannie care,
  And no neglect.

[1] A *song* he had promised the Author.

Tho', faith, sma' heart hae I to sing!
My Muse dow scarcely spread her wing!
I've play'd mysel a bonie *spring*,
      An' *danc'd* my fill!
I'd better gaen an' sair't the king,
      At Bunker's Hill.

'Twas ae night lately, in my fun,
I gaed a roving wi' the gun,
An' brought a *Paitrick* to the *grun*,
      A bonie *hen*,
And, as the twilight was begun,
      Thought nane wad ken.

The poor, wee thing was *little hurt;*
I *straikit it* a wee for sport,
Ne'er thinkin they wad fash me for't;
      But, Deil-ma-care!
Somebody tells the *Poacher-Court*
      The hale affair.

Some auld, us'd hands had ta'en a note,
That *sic a hen* had got a *shot;*
I was suspected for the plot;
      I scorn'd to lie;
So gat the whissle o my groat
      An' pay't the *fee.*

But, by my *gun*, o' guns the wale,
An' by my *pouther* an' my *hale*,
An' by my *hen*, an' by her *tail*,
  I vow an' swear!
The *Game* shall pay, o'er moor an' *dail*
  For this, niest year.

As soon's the *clockin-time* is by,
An' the *wee powts* begun to cry,
Lord, I'se hae sportin by an' by,
  For my *gowd guinea*;
Tho' I should herd the *buckskin* kye
  For't, in Virginia!

Trowth, they had muckle for to blame!
'Twas neither broken wing nor limb,
But twa-three *draps* about the *wame*
  Scarce thro' the *feathers*;
An' baith a *yellow George* to claim,
  An' *thole* their *blethers*!

It pits me aye as mad's a hare;
So I can rhyme nor write nae mair;
But *pennyworths* again is fair,
  When time's expedient:
Meanwhile I am, respected Sir,
  Your most obedient.

LAMENT FOR JAMES, EARL OF GLENCAIRN.

THE wind blew hollow frae the hills,
   By fits the sun's departing beam
Look'd on the fading yellow woods
   That wav'd o'er Lugar's winding stream:
Beneath a craigy steep, a Bard,
   Laden with years and meikle pain,
In loud lament bewail'd his lord,
   Whom death had all untimely taen.

He lean'd him to an ancient aik,
   Whose trunk was mould'ring down with years;
His locks were bleached white wi' time,
   His hoary cheek was wet wi' tears;
And as he touch'd his trembling harp,
   And as he tun'd his doleful sang,
The winds, lamenting thro' their caves,
   To echo bore the notes alang.

"Ye scatter'd birds that faintly sing,
   The reliques of the vernal quire;
Ye woods that shed on a' the winds
   The honours of the aged year,

A few short months, and glad and gay,
   Again ye'll charm the ear and e'e;
But nocht in all-revolving time
   Can gladness bring again to me.

"I am a bending aged tree,
   That long has stood the wind and rain;
But now has come a cruel blast,
   And my last hold of earth is gane:
Nae leaf o' mine shall greet the spring,
   Nae simmer sun exalt my bloom;
But I maun lie before the storm,
   And ithers plant them in my room.

"I've seen sae mony changfu' years,
   On earth I am a stranger grown;
I wander in the ways of men,
   Alike unknowing and unknown:
Unheard, unpitied, unreliev'd,
   I bear alane my lade o' care,
For silent, low, on beds of dust,
   Lie a' that would my sorrows share.

"And last (the sum of a' my griefs!)
   My noble master lies in clay;
The flow'r amang our barons bold,
   His country's pride, his country's stay:

In weary being now I pine,
    For a' the life of life is dead,
And hope has left my aged ken,
    On forward wing for ever fled.

"Awake thy last sad voice, my harp!
    The voice of woe and wild despair!
Awake, resound thy latest lay,
    Then sleep in silence evermair!
And thou, my last, best, only friend,
    That fillest an untimely tomb,
Accept this tribute from the Bard
    Thou brought from fortune's mirkest gloom.

"In Poverty's low barren vale,
    Thick mists, obscure, involv'd me round;
Though oft I turn'd the wistful eye,
    Nae ray of fame was to be found:
Thou found'st me, like the morning sun
    That melts the fogs in limpid air,
The friendless Bard and rustic song,
    Became alike thy fostering care.

"O! why has Worth so short a date!
    While villains ripen grey with time!
Must thou, the noble, generous, great,
    Fall in bold manhood's hardy prime!

Why did I live to see that day?
A day to me so full of woe?
O! had I met the mortal shaft
Which laid my benefactor low!

"The bridegroom may forget the bride,
Was made his wedded wife yestreen;
The monarch may forget the crown
That on his head an hour has been;
The mother may forget the child
That smiles sae sweetly on her knee;
But I'll remember thee, Glencairn,
And a' that thou hast done for me!"

TAM O' SHANTER.

A TALE.

Of Brownyis and of Bogilis full in this Buke.
                                   GAWIN DOUGLAS.

WHEN chapman billies leave the street,
   And drouthy neebors, neebors meet,
As market-days are wearing late,
An' folk begin to tak the gate;
While we sit bousing at the nappy,
An' getting fou and unco happy,

We think na on the lang Scots miles,
The mosses, waters, slaps, and styles,
That lie between us and our hame,
Whare sits our sulky sullen dame,
Gathering her brows like gathering storm,
Nursing her wrath to keep it warm.

This truth fand honest *Tam o' Shanter*,
As he frae Ayr ae night did canter,
(Auld Ayr, wham ne'er a town surpasses,
For honest men and bonny lasses.)

O *Tam!* hadst thou but been sae wise,
As ta'en thy ain wife *Kate's* advice!
She tauld thee weel thou wast a skellum,
A blethering, blustering, drunken blellum;
That frae November till October,
Ae market-day thou was nae sober;
That ilka melder, wi' the miller,
Thou sat as lang as thou had siller;
That ev'ry naig was ca'd a shoe on,
The smith and thee gat roaring fou on;
That at the Lord's house, ev'n on Sunday,
Thou drank wi' Kirton Jean till Monday.
She prophesy'd that late, or soon,
Thou would be found deep drown'd in Doon;
Or catch'd wi' warlocks in the mirk,
By *Alloway's* auld haunted kirk.

Ah, gentle dames! it gars me greet,
To think how mony counsels sweet,
How mony lengthen'd sage advices,
The husband frae the wife despises!

But to our tale: Ae market night,
Tam had got planted unco right;
Fast by an ingle, bleezing finely,
Wi' reaming swats, that drank divinely;
And at his elbow, Souter *Johnny*,
His ancient, trusty, drouthy crony;
Tam lo'ed him like a vera brither;
They had been fou for weeks thegither.
The night drave on wi' sangs and clatter;
And ay the ale was growing better:
The landlady and *Tam* grew gracious,
Wi' favours, secret, sweet, and precious:
The Souter tauld his queerest stories;
The landlord's laugh was ready chorus:
The storm without might rair and rustle,
Tam did na mind the storm a whistle.

Care, mad to see a man sae happy,
E'en drown'd himsel amang the nappy:
As bees flee hame wi' lades o' treasure,
The minutes wing'd their way wi' pleasure;
Kings may be blest, but *Tam* was glorious,
O'er the ills o' life victorious!

But pleasures are like poppies spread,
You seize the flow'r, its bloom is shed;
Or like the snow-falls in the river,
A moment white—then melts for ever;
Or like the borealis race,
That flit ere you can point their place;
Or like the rainbow's lovely form
Evanishing amid the storm.—
Nae man can tether time or tide;—
The hour approaches *Tam* maun ride;
That hour, o' night's black arch the key-stane,
That dreary hour he mounts his beast in;
And sic a night he taks the road in,
As ne'er poor sinner was abroad in.

The wind blew as 'twad blawn its last;
The rattling show'rs rose on the blast;
The speedy gleams the darkness swallow'd;
Loud, deep, and lang, the thunder bellow'd:
That night, a child might understand,
The Deil had business on his hand.

Weel mounted on his grey mare, *Meg*,
A better never lifted leg,
Tam skelpit on thro' dub and mire,
Despising wind, and rain, and fire;
Whiles holding fast his gude blue bonnet;
Whiles crooning o'er some auld Scots sonnet;

Whiles glow'ring round wi' prudent cares,
Lest bogles catch him unawares:
Kirk-Alloway was drawing nigh,
Whare ghaists and houlets nightly cry.—

By this time he was cross the ford,
Whare in the snaw, the chapman smoor'd;
And past the birks and meikle stane,
Whare drunken *Charlie* brak's neck-bane;
And thro' the whins, and by the cairn,
Whare hunters fand the murder'd bairn;
And near the thorn, aboon the well,
Whare *Mungo's* mither hang'd hersel.—
Before him *Doon* pours all his floods;
The doubling storm roars thro' the woods;
The lightnings flash from pole to pole;
Near and more near the thunders roll:
When, glimmering thro' the groaning trees,
Kirk-Alloway seem'd in a bleeze;
Thro' ilka bore the beams were glancing;
And loud resounded mirth and dancing.—

Inspiring bold *John Barleycorn!*
What dangers thou canst make us scorn!
Wi' tippenny, we fear nae evil;
Wi' usquebae, we'll face the devil!—
The swats sae ream'd in *Tammie's* noodle,
Fair play, he car'd na deils a boddle.

But *Maggie* stood right sair astonish'd,
Till, by the heel and hand admonish'd,
She ventur'd forward on the light;
And, vow! *Tam* saw an unco sight!
Warlocks and witches in a dance;
Nae cotillion brent new frae *France*
But hornpipes, jigs, strathspeys, and reels,
Put life and mettle in their heels.
A winnock-bunker in the east,
There sat auld Nick, in shape o' beast;
A towzie tyke, black, grim, and large,
To gie them music was his charge:
He screw'd the pipes and gart them skirl,
Till roof and rafters a' did dirl.—
Coffins stood round like open presses,
That shaw'd the dead in their last dresses;
And by some devilish cantraip slight
Each in its cauld hand held a light,—
By which heroic *Tam* was able
To note upon the haly table,
A murderer's banes in gibbet airns;
Twa span-lang, wee, unchristen'd bairns;
A thief, new-cutted frae the rape,
Wi' his last gasp his gab did gape;
Five tomahawks, wi' blude red rusted;
Five scymitars, wi' murder crusted;
A garter, which a babe had strangled;

A knife, a father's throat had mangled,
Whom his ain son o' life bereft,
The grey hairs yet stack to the heft;
Wi' mair o' horrible and awefu',
Which even to name wad be unlawfu'.

    As *Tammie* glowr'd, amaz'd, and curious,
The mirth and fun grew fast and furious:
The piper loud and louder blew;
The dancers quick and quicker flew;
They reel'd, they set, they cross'd, they cleekit,
Till ilka carlin swat and reekit,
And coost her duddies to the wark,
And linket at it in her sark!

    Now *Tam*, O *Tam!* had thae been queans,
A' plump and strapping in their teens;
Their sarks, instead o' creeshie flannen,
Been snaw-white seventeen hunder linnen!
Thir breeks o' mine, my only pair,
That ance were plush, o' gude blue hair,
I wad hae gi'en them off my hurdies,
For ae blink o' the bonie burdies!

    But wither'd beldams, auld and droll,
Rigwoodie hags wad spean a foal,
Lowping and flinging on a crummock,
I wonder didna turn thy stomach.

But *Tam* kend what was what fu' brawlie,
There was ae winsome wench and wawlie,
That night enlisted in the core,
(Lang after kend on *Carrick* shore;
For mony a beast to dead she shot,
And perish'd mony a bony boat,
And shook baith meikle corn and bear,
And kept the country-side in fear,)
Her cutty sark, o' Paisley harn,
That while a lassie she had worn,
In longitude tho' sorely scanty,
It was her best, and she was vauntie.—
Ah! little kend thy reverend grannie,
That sark she coft for her wee Nannie,
Wi' twa pund Scots ('twas a' her riches),
Wad ever grac'd a dance of witches!

But here my Muse her wing maun cour;
Sic flights are far beyond her pow'r;
To sing how Nannie lap and flang,
(A souple jade she was, and strang,)
And how *Tam* stood, like ane bewitch'd,
And thought his very een enrich'd;
Even Satan glowr'd, and fidg'd fu' fain,
And hotch'd and blew wi' might and main:
Till first ae caper, syne anither,
Tam tint his reason a' thegither,

And roars out, "Weel done, Cutty-sark!"
And in an instant all was dark:
And scarcely had he Maggie rallied,
When out the hellish legion sallied.

As bees bizz out wi' angry fyke,
When plundering herds assail their byke;
As open pussie's mortal foes,
When, pop! she starts before their nose;
As eager runs the market-crowd,
When, "Catch the thief!" resounds aloud;
So Maggie runs, the witches follow,
Wi' mony an eldritch skreech and hollow.

Ah, *Tam!* ah, *Tam!* thou'll get thy fairin!
In hell they'll roast thee like an herrin!
In vain thy *Kate* awaits thy comin!
Kate soon will be a woefu' woman!
Now, do thy speedy utmost, Meg,
And win the key-stane[1] of the brig:
There at them thou thy tail may toss,
A running stream they darena cross.

---

[1] It is a well-known fact that witches, or any evil spirits, have no power to follow a poor wight any further than the middle of the next running stream. It may be proper likewise to mention to the benighted traveller, that when he falls in with *bogles*, whatever danger may be in his going forward, there is much more hazard in turning back.

But ere the key-stane she could make,
The fient a tail she had to shake!
For Nannie, far before the rest,
Hard upon noble Maggie prest,
And flew at Tam wi' furious ettle;
But little wist she Maggie's mettle—
Ae spring brought off her master hale,
But left behind her ain gray tail:
The carlin claught her by the rump,
And left poor Maggie scarce a stump.

Now, wha this tale o' truth shall read,
Ilk man and mother's son, take heed:
Whene'er to drink you are inclin'd,
Or cutty-sarks run in your mind,
Think, ye may buy the joys o'er dear,
Remember Tam o' Shanter's mare.

ON THE LATE CAPTAIN GROSE'S PEREGRINATIONS THRO' SCOTLAND,

COLLECTING THE ANTIQUITIES OF THAT KINGDOM.

HEAR, Land o' Cakes, and brither Scots,
    Frae Maidenkirk to Johnny Groats!—
If there's a hole in a' your coats,
      I rede you tent it:
A child's amang you, taking notes,
      And, faith, he'll prent it.

If in your bounds ye chance to light
Upon a fine, fat, fodgel wight,
O' stature short, but genius bright,
      That's he, mark weel—
And wow! he has an unco slight
      O' cauk and keel.

By some auld, houlet-haunted, biggin,[1]
Or kirk deserted by its riggin,
It's ten to ane ye'll find him snug in
      Some eldritch part,
Wi' deils, they say, Lord save's! colleaguin
      At some black art.—

[1] *Vide* his "Antiquities of Scotland."

Ilk ghaist that haunts auld ha' or chamer,
Ye gipsy-gang that deal in glamor,
And you, deep-read in hell's black grammar,
    Warlocks and witches;
Ye'll quake at his conjuring hammer,
    Ye midnight bitches.

It's tauld he was a sodger bred,
And ane wad rather fa'n than fled;
But now he's quat the spurtle-blade,
    And dog-skin wallet,
And taen the—*Antiquarian trade*,
    I think they call it.

He has a fouth o' auld nick-nackets:
Rusty airn caps and jinglin jackets,[1]
Wad haud the Lothians three in tackets,
    A towmont gude;
And parritch-pats, and auld saut-backets,
    Before the Flood.

Of Eve's first fire he has a cinder;
Auld Tubalcain's fire-shool and fender;
That which distinguished the gender
    O' Balaam's ass;
A broom-stick o' the witch of Endor,
    Weel shod wi' brass.

---

[1] *Vide* his treatise on ancient armour and weapons.

Forbye, he'll shape you aff, fu' gleg
The cut of Adam's philibeg;
The knife that nicket Abel's craig
   He'll prove you fully,
It was a faulding jocteleg,
   Or lang-kail gullie.—

But wad ye see him in his glee,
For meikle glee and fun has he,
Then set him down, and twa or three
   Gude fellows wi' him;
And *port*, O *port!* shine thou a wee,
   And THEN ye'll see him!

Now, by the Pow'rs o' Verse and Prose!
Thou art a dainty chield, O Grose!—
Whae'er o' thee shall ill suppose,
   They sair misca' thee;
I'd take the rascal by the nose,
   Wad say, Shame fa' thee.

VERSES WRITTEN UNDER THE PORTRAIT OF FERGUSSON THE POET,

IN A COPY OF THAT AUTHOR'S WORKS PRESENTED TO A YOUNG LADY IN EDINBURGH, MARCH 19TH, 1787.

CURSE on ungrateful man, that can be pleas'd,
And yet can starve the author of the pleasure.
O thou, my elder brother in misfortune,
By far my elder brother in the muses,
With tears I pity thy unhappy fate!
Why is the bard unpitied by the world,
Yet has so keen a relish of its pleasures?

VERSES

ON THE DESTRUCTION OF THE WOODS NEAR DRUMLANRIG.

AS on the banks o' wandering Nith,
Ae smiling simmer-morn I stray'd,
And traced its bonnie howes and haughs,
Where linties sang and lambkins play'd.

I sat me down upon a craig,
    And drank my fill o' fancy's dream,
When, from the eddying deep below,
    Uprose the genius of the stream.

Dark, like the frowning rock, his brow,
    And troubled, like his wintry wave,
And deep, as sughs the boding wind
    Amang his eaves, the sigh he gave—
"And came ye here, my son," he cried,
    "To wander in my birken shade?
To muse some favourite Scottish theme,
    Or sing some favourite Scottish maid.

"There was a time, it's nae lang syne,
    Ye might hae seen me in my pride,
When a' my banks sae bravely saw
    Their woody pictures in my tide;
When hanging beech and spreading elm
    Shaded my stream sae clear and cool;
And stately oaks their twisted arms
    Threw broad and dark across the pool;

"When, glinting through the trees, appear'd
    The wee white cot aboon the mill,
And peacefu' rose its ingle reek,
    That slowly curled up the hill.

But now the cot is bare and cauld,
　　Its branchy shelter's lost and gane,
And scarce a stinted birk is left
　　To shiver in the blast its lane."

"Alas!" said I, "what ruefu' chance
　　Has twined ye o' your stately trees?
Has laid your rocky bosom bare?
　　Has stripp'd the cleading o' your braes?—
Was it the bitter eastern blast,
　　That scatters blight in early spring?
Or was't the wil'fire scorch'd their boughs,
　　Or canker-worm wi' secret sting?"

"Nae eastlan' blast," the sprite replied;
　　"It blew na here sae fierce and fell,
And on my dry and halesome banks
　　Nae canker-worms get leave to dwell:
Man! cruel man!" the genius sigh'd—
　　As through the cliffs he sank him down,—
"The worm that gnaw'd my bonnie trees,
　　That reptile wears a ducal crown."

THE SOLEMN LEAGUE AND COVENANT.

THE Solemn League and Covenant
    Cost Scotland blood—cost Scotland tears:
But it seal'd freedom's sacred cause—
    If thou'rt a slave, indulge thy sneers.

THERE'S NAETHIN LIKE THE HONEST NAPPY.

THERE'S naethin like the honest nappy!
    Whaur'll ye e'er see men sae happy,
Or women sonsie, saft an' sappy,
        'Tween morn an' morn,
As them wha like to taste the drappie
        In glass or horn.

I've seen me daez't upon a time;
I scarce could wink or see a styme;
Just ae hauf muchkin does me prime,
        Ought less is little,
Then back I rattle on the rhyme
        As gleg's a whittle!

SONGS.

SONGS.

MY AIN KIND DEARIE O.

WHEN o'er the hill the eastern star,
    Tells bughtin-time is near, my jo;
And owsen frae the furrow'd field
    Return sae dowf and wearie O;
Down by the burn, where scented birks
    Wi' dew are hanging clear, my jo,
I'll meet thee on the lea-rig,
    My ain kind dearie O.

In mirkest glen, at midnight hour,
    I'd rove, and ne'er be eerie O,
If thro' that glen I gaed to thee,
    My ain kind dearie O.
Altho' the night were ne'er sae wild,
    And I were ne'er sae wearie O,
I'd meet thee on the lea-rig,
    My ain kind dearie O.

The hunter lo'es the morning sun,
    To rouse the mountain deer, my jo ;
At noon the fisher seeks the glen,
    Alang the burn to steer, my jo ;
Gie me the hour o' gloamin' grey,
    It maks my heart sae cheery O,
To meet thee on the lea-rig,
    My ain kind dearie O.

AULD ROB MORRIS.

THERE'S auld Rob Morris that wons in yon glen,
    He's the king o' gude fellows, and wale of auld men ;
He has gowd in his coffers, he has sheep, he has kine,
And ae bonie lassie, his darling and mine.

She's fresh as the morning, the fairest in May ;
She's sweet as the ev'ning amang the new hay ;
As blythe and as artless as the lamb on the lea,
And dear to my heart as the light to my e'e.

But oh ! she's an heiress, auld Robin's a laird,
And my daddie has nought but a cot-house and yard :
A wooer like me maunna hope to come speed ;
The wounds I maun hide that will soon be my dead.

The day comes to me, but delight brings me nane;
The night comes to me, but my rest it is gane:
I wander my lane, like a night-troubled ghaist,
And I sigh as my heart it would burst in my breast.

O had she but been of a lower degree,
I then might hae hop'd she wad smil'd upon me!
O, how past descriving had then been my bliss,
As now my distraction no words can express!

MY WIFE'S A WINSOME WEE THING.

SHE is a winsome wee thing,
   She is a handsome wee thing,
She is a bonie wee thing,
This sweet wee wife o' mine.

I never saw a fairer,
I never loe'd a dearer,
And neist my heart I'll wear her,
For fear my jewel tine.

She is a winsome wee thing,
She is a handsome wee thing,
She is a bonie wee thing,
This sweet wee wife o' mine.

The world's wrack, we share o't,
The warstle and the care o't;
Wi' her I'll blythely bear it,
And think my lot divine.

DUNCAN GRAY CAM' HERE TO WOO.

DUNCAN Gray cam' here to woo,
    Ha, ha, the wooing o't,
On blyth yule-night when we were fu',
    Ha, ha, the wooing o't.
MAGGIE coost her head fu' high,
Look'd asklent and unco skeigh,
Gart poor Duncan stand abeigh;
    Ha, ha, the wooing o't.

Duncan fleech'd and Duncan pray'd;
    Ha, ha, the wooing o't,
Meg was deaf as AILSA CRAIG,
    Ha, ha, the wooing o't.
Duncan sigh'd, both out and in,
Grat his een baith bleer't and blin',
Spak o' lowping o'er a linn;
    Ha, ha, the wooing o't.

Time and chance are but a tide,
  Ha, ha, the wooing o't.
Slighted love is sair to bide,
  Ha, ha, the wooing o't.
Shall I, like a fool, quoth he,
For a haughty hizzie die?
She may gae to—France for me!
  Ha, ha, the wooing o't.

How it comes, let Doctors tell,
  Ha, ha, the wooing o't;
Meg grew sick,—as he grew hale,
  Ha, ha, the wooing o't.
Something in her bosom wrings,
For relief a sigh she brings;
And oh! her een they spak sic things!
  Ha, ha, the wooing o't.

Duncan was a lad o' grace,
  Ha, ha, the wooing o't;
Maggie's was a piteous case,
  Ha, ha, the wooing o't.
Duncan cou'dna be her death,
Swelling pity smoor'd his wrath;
Now—they're crouse and canty baith!
  Ha, ha, the wooing o't.

BRAW LADS ON YARROW BRAES.

BRAW, braw lads on Yarrow braes,
    Ye wander thro' the blooming heather;
But Yarrow braes, nor Ettrick shaws,
    Can match the lads o' Galla Water.

But there is ane, a secret ane,
    Aboon them a' I loo him better:
And I'll be his, and he'll be mine,
    The bonnie lad o' Galla Water.

Altho' his daddie was nae laird,
    And tho' I hae na meikle tocher;
Yet rich in kindest, truest love,
    We'll tent our flocks by Galla Water.

It ne'er was wealth, it ne'er was wealth,
    That coft contentment, peace, or pleasure;
The bands and bliss o' mutual love,
    O that's the warld's chiefest treasure!

WANDERING WILLIE.

HERE awa, there awa, wandering WILLIE,
  Here awa, there awa, haud awa hame;
Come to my bosom, my ain only dearie,
  Tell me thou bring'st me my WILLIE the same.

Winter winds blew, loud and cauld, at our parting,
  Fears for my WILLIE brought tears in my ee;
Welcome now Simmer, and welcome my WILLIE,
  The Simmer to Nature, my WILLIE to me.

Rest, ye wild storms, in the cave of your slumbers;
  How your dread howling a lover alarms!
Wauken, ye breezes! row gently, ye billows!
  And waft my dear Laddie ance mair to my arms.

But oh, if he's faithless, and minds na his NANIE,
  Flow still between us thou wide-roaring main;
May I never see it, may I never trow it,
  But, dying, believe that my WILLIE'S my ain!

LOGAN BRAES.

Tune—"*Logan Water.*"

O, LOGAN, sweetly didst thou glide,
   That day I was my Willie's bride;
And years sinsyne hae o'er us run,
Like Logan to the simmer sun.
But now thy flow'ry banks appear
Like Drumlie winter, dark and drear,
While my dear lad maun face his faes,
Far, far frae me and Logan Braes.

Again the merry month o' May
Has made our hills and vallies gay;
The birds rejoice in leafy bowers,
The bees hum round the breathing flowers:
Blithe morning lifts his rosy eye,
And evening's tears are tears of joy:
My soul, delightless, a' surveys,
While Willie's far frae Logan Braes.

Within yon milk-white hawthorn bush,
Amang her nestlings sits the thrush;
Her faithfu' mate will share her toil,
Or wi' his song her cares beguile:

But I wi' my sweet nurslings here,
Nae mate to help, nae mate to cheer,
Pass widow'd nights and joyless days,
While Willie's far frae Logan Braes.

O wae upon you, men o' state,
That brethren rouse to deadly hate!
As ye mak mony a fond heart mourn,
Sae may it on your heads return!
How can your flinty hearts enjoy
The widow's tears, the orphan's cry?
But soon may peace bring happy days,
And Willie, hame to Logan Braes!

O LASSIE, ART THOU SLEEPING YET?

TUNE—"*Let me in this ae night.*"

O LASSIE, art thou sleeping yet?
    Or art thou waking? I would wit,
For love has bound me, hand and foot,
    And I would fain be in, jo.

CHORUS.
O let me in this ae night,
    This ae, ae, ae night;
For pity's sake this ae night,
    O rise and let me in, jo.

Thou hear'st the winter wind and weet,
Nae star blinks thro' the driving sleet;
Tak pity on my weary feet,
    And shield me frae the rain, jo.
        O let me in, etc.

The bitter blast that round me blaws,
Unheeded howls, unheeded fa's;
The cauldness o' thy heart's the cause
    Of a' my grief and pain, jo.
        O let me in, etc.

HER ANSWER.

O TELL na me o' wind and rain,
Upbraid na me wi' cauld disdain,
Gae back the gate ye cam again,
 I winna let you in, jo.

CHORUS.

 I tell you now this ae night,
  This ae, ae, ae night;
 And ance for a' this ae night,
  I winna let you in, jo.

The snellest blast, at mirkest hours,
That round the pathless wand'rer pours,
Is nocht to what poor she endures,
 That's trusted faithless man, jo.
  I tell you now, etc.

The sweetest flower that deck'd the mead,
Now trodden like the vilest weed:
Let simple maid the lesson read,
 The weird may be her ain, jo.
  I tell you now, etc.

The bird that charm'd his summer-day,
Is now the cruel fowler's prey;
Let witless, trusting, woman say
 How aft her fate's the same, jo.
  I tell you now, etc.

GROVES O' SWEET MYRTLE.

TUNE—"*Humours of glen.*"

THEIR groves o' sweet myrtle let foreign lands reckon,
   Where bright beaming-summers exalt the perfume;
Far dearer to me yon lone glen o' green breckan,
   Wi' the burn stealing under the lang, yellow broom:
Far dearer to me are yon humble broom bowers,
   Where the blue-bell and gowan lurk, lowly, unseen;
For there, lightly tripping amang the wild flowers,
   A-listening the linnet, aft wanders my JEAN.

Tho' rich is the breeze in *their* gay sunny vallies,
   And cauld, Caledonia's blast on the wave;
Their sweet-scented woodlands that skirt the proud palace,
   What are they?—The haunt of the Tyrant and Slave!
The Slave's spicy forests, and gold-bubbling fountains,
   The brave Caledonian views wi' disdain;
He wanders as free as the winds of his mountains,
   Save LOVE's willing fetters, the chains o' his JEAN.

LAST MAY A BRAW WOOER CAM' DOWN THE LANG GLEN.

TUNE—"*Lothian Lassie.*"

LAST May a braw wooer cam down the lang glen,
    And sair wi' his love he did deave me;
I said, there was naething I hated like men,
    The deuce gae wi' him to believe me, believe me,
    The deuce gae wi' him to believe me.

He spak o' the darts in my bonie black een,
    And vow'd for my love he was dying;
I said he might die when he liked for Jean;
    The Lord forgie me for lying, for lying,
    The Lord forgie me for lying!

A weel-stocked mailen, himsel for the laird,
    And marriage aff hand, were his proffers:
I never loot on that I kend it, or car'd,
    But thought I might hae waur offers, waur offers,
    But thought I might hae waur offers.

But what wad ye think? in a fortnight or less,—
    The deil tak his taste to gae near her!—
He up the lang loan to my black cousin Bess,

Guess ye how the jad ! I could bear her, could bear her,
Guess ye how the jad ! I could bear her.

But a' the niest week as I petted wi' care,
  I gaed to the tryste o' Dalgarnock ;
And wha but my fine fickle lover was there,
    I glowr'd as I'd seen a warlock, a warlock,
    I glowr'd as I'd seen a warlock.

But owre my left shouther I ga'e him a blink,
  Lest neebors might say I was saucy :
My wooer he caper'd as he'd been in drink,
    And vow'd I was his dear lassie, dear lassie,
    And vow'd I was his dear lassie.

I spier'd for my cousin fu' couthy and sweet,
  If she had recover'd her hearing ;
And how her new shoon fit her auld shachl't feet ;
    But, heavens ! how he fell a-swearing, a-swearing,
    But, heavens ! how he fell a-swearing.

He begged, for gude-sake ! I wad be his wife,
  Or else I wad kill him wi' sorrow :
So e'en to preserve the poor body in life,
    I think I maun wed him—to-morrow, to-morrow,
    I think I maun wed him to-morrow.

BLYTHE WAS SHE.

Tune—"*Andro and his cuttie gun.*"

CHORUS.
Blythe, Blythe and merry was she,
   Blythe was she but and ben :
Blythe by the banks of Ern,
   And blythe in Glenturit glen.

BY Ochtertyre grows the aik,
   On Yarrow banks, the birken shaw;
But Phemie was a bonier lass
   Than braes o' Yarrow ever saw.
      Blythe, etc.

Her looks were like a flow'r in May,
   Her smile was like a simmer morn;
She tripped by the banks of Ern,
   As light's a bird upon a thorn.
      Blythe, etc.

Her bonie face it was as meek
   As ony lamb upon a lee;
The evening sun was ne'er sae sweet
   As was the blink o' Phemie's e'e.
      Blythe, etc.

The Highland hills I've wander'd wide,
    And o'er the Lawlands I hae been ;
But Phemie was the blythest lass
    That ever trode the dewy green.
        Blythe, &c.

I LOVE MY JEAN.

TUNE—"*Mrs. Admiral Gordon's Strathspey.*"

O A' the airts the wind can blaw,
    I dearly like the west,
For there the bonie Lassie lives,
    The Lassie I lo'e best :
There wild-woods grow, and rivers row,
    And mony a hill between ;
But day and night my fancy's flight
    Is ever wi' my Jean.

I see her in the dewy flowers,
    I see her sweet and fair ;
I hear her in the tunefu' birds,
    I hear her charm the air :
There's not a bonie flower that springs
    By fountain, shaw, or green,
There's not a bonie bird that sings,
    But minds me o' my Jean.

WILLIE BREW'D A PECK O' MAUT.

O WILLIE brew'd a peck o' maut,
    And Rob and Allan cam to see;
Three blyther hearts, that lee-lang night,
    Ye wad na find in Christendie.

CHORUS.
We are na fou, we're nae that fou,
    But just a drappie in our e'e;
The cock may craw, the day may daw,
    And ay we'll taste the barley bree.

Here are we met, three merry boys,
    Three merry boys I trow are we;
And mony a night we've merry been,
    And mony mae we hope to be!
        We are na fou, etc.

It is the moon, I ken her horn,
    That's blinkin in the lift sae hie;
She shines sae bright to wyle us hame,
    But by my sooth she'll wait a wee!
        We are na fou, etc.

Wha first shall rise to gang awa,
   A cuckold, coward loun is he !
Wha last beside his chair shall fa',
   He is the king among us three !
     We are na fou, etc.

JOHN ANDERSON MY JO.

JOHN ANDERSON my jo, John,
   When we were first Acquent ;
Your locks were like the raven,
   Your bony brow was brent ;
But now your brow is beld, John,
   Your locks are like the snaw ;
But blessings on your frosty pow,
   John Anderson my Jo.

John Anderson my jo, John,
   We clamb the hill thegither ;
And mony a canty day John,
   We've had wi' ane anither :
Now we maun totter down, John,
   But hand in hand we'll go ;
And sleep thegither at the foot,
   John Anderson my Jo.

GUIDWIFE COUNT THE LAWIN.

GANE is the day and mirk's the night,
But we'll ne'er stray for faute o' light,
For ale and brandy's stars and moon,
And bluid-red wine's the risin' Sun.

CHORUS.
Then guidwife count the lawin, the lawin, the lawin,
Then guidwife count the lawin, and bring a coggie
  mair.

There's wealth and ease for gentlemen,
And semple-folk maun fecht and fen',
But here we're a' in ae accord,
For ilka man that's drunk's a lord.
 Then guidwife count, etc.

My coggie is a haly pool,
That heals the wounds o' care and dool;
And pleasure is a wanton trout,
An' ye drink it a', ye'll find him out.
 Then guidwife count, etc.

WHAT CAN A YOUNG LASSIE DO WI' AN AULD MAN.

Tune—" What can a Lassie do."

WHAT can a young lassie, what shall a young lassie,
   What can a young lassie do wi' an auld man?
Bad luck on the pennie that tempted my Minnie
   To sell her poor Jenny for siller an' lan'!

He's always compleenin frae mornin to e'enin,
   He hosts and he hirples the weary day lang:
He's doylt and he's dozin, his bluid it is frozen,
   O, dreary's the night wi' a crazy auld man!

He hums and he hankers, he frets and he cankers,
   I never can please him, do a' that I can;
He's peevish, and jealous of a' the young fellows,
   O, dool on the day I met wi' an auld man!

My auld auntie Katie upon me takes pity,
   I'll do my endeavour to follow her plan;
I'll cross him, and wrack him, until I heart-break him,
   And then his auld brass will buy me a new pan.

O, FOR ANE AND TWENTY, TAM!

Tune—"*The Moudiewort.*"

CHORUS.

An O, for ane and twenty, Tam !
   An hey, sweet ane and twenty, Tam !
I'll learn my kin a rattlin sang,
   An I saw ane and twenty, Tam.

THEY snool me sair, and haud me down,
   And gar me look like bluntie, Tam ;
But three short years will soon wheel roun',
   And then comes ane and twenty, Tam.
   An O, for ane and twenty, Tam !
      An hey, sweet ane and twenty, Tam !
   I'll learn my kin a rattlin sang,
      An I saw ane and twenty, Tam.

A gleib o' lan', a claut o' gear,
   Was left me by my Auntie, Tam ;
At kith or kin I need na spier,
   An I saw ane and twenty, Tam.

An O, for ane and twenty, Tam !
An hey, sweet ane and twenty, Tam !
I'll learn my kin a rattlin sang,
An I saw ane and twenty, Tam.

They'll hae me wed a wealthy coof,
Tho' I mysel hae plenty, Tam ;
But hear'st thou, laddie, there's my loof,
I'm thine at ane and twenty, Tam !
An O, for ane and twenty, Tam !
An hey, sweet ane and twenty, Tam !
I'll learn my kin a rattlin sang,
An I saw ane and twenty, Tam.

BESS AND HER SPINNING WHEEL.

TUNE—"*Bottom of the Punch Bowl.*"

O LEEZE me on my spinning wheel,
   And leeze me on my rock and reel ;
Frae tap to tae that cleeds me bien,
And haps me fiel and warm at e'en !
I'll set me down and sing and spin,
While laigh descends the simmer sun,
Blest wi' content, and milk and meal—
O leeze me on my spinnin wheel.

On ilka hand the burnies trot,
And meet below my theekit cot;
The scented birk and hawthorn white
Across the pool their arms unite,
Alike to screen the birdie's nest,
And little fishes' caller rest :
The sun blinks kindly in the biel',
Where, blythe I turn my spinnin wheel.

On lofty aiks the cushats wail,
And Echo cons the doolfu' tale;
The lintwhites in the hazel braes,
Delighted, rival ither's lays :
The craik amang the claver hay,
The paitrick whirrin o'er the ley,
The swallow jinkin round my shiel,
Amuse me at my spinnin wheel.

Wi' sma' to sell, and less to buy,
Aboon distress, below envy,
O wha wad leave this humble state,
For a' the pride of a' the great?
Amid their flaring, idle toys,
Amid their cumbrous, dinsome joys,
Can they the peace and pleasure feel
Of Bessy at her spinnin wheel?

THE BANKS O' DOON.

Tune—"*The Caledonian Hunt's delight.*"

YE Banks and braes o' bonie Doon,
   How can ye bloom sae fresh and fair !
How can ye chant, ye little birds,
   And I sae weary, fu' o' care !
Thou'lt break my heart thou warbling bird,
   That wantons thro' the flowering thorn :
Thou minds me o' departed joys,
   Departed—never to return.

Aft hae I rov'd by bonie Doon,
   To see the rose and woodbine twine ;
And ilka bird sang o' its luve,
   And fondly sae did I o' mine.
Wi' lightsome heart I pu'd a rose,
   Fu' sweet upon its thorny tree ;
And my fause luver stole my rose,
   But ah ! he left the thorn wi' me.

VERSION PRINTED IN THE MUSICAL MUSEUM.

YE flowery banks o' bonie Doon,
    How can ye blume sae fair;
How can ye chant, ye little birds,
    And I sae fu' o' care!

Thou'll break my heart, thou bonie bird,
    That sings upon the bough;
Thou minds me o' the happy days
    When my fause luve was true.

Thou'll break my heart, thou bonie bird,
    That sings beside thy mate;
For sae I sat, and sae I sang,
    And wist na o' my fate.

Aft hae I rov'd by bonie Doon,
    To see the wood-bine twine,
And ilka bird sang o' its love,
    And sae did I o' mine.

Wi' lightsome heart I pu'd a rose
Frae off its thorny tree ;
And my fause luver staw the rose,
But left the thorn wi' me.

FOR THE SAKE O' SOMEBODY.

TUNE—"*The Highland Watch's farewell.*"

MY heart is sair, I dare na tell,
   My heart is sair for Somebody ;
I could wake a winter night,
  For the sake o' Somebody !
    Oh-hon ! for Somebody !
    Oh-hey ! for Somebody !
I could range the world around
For the sake o' Somebody !

Ye Powers that smile on virtuous love,
  O, sweetly smile on Somebody !
Frae ilka danger keep him free,
  And send me safe my Somebody.
    Oh-hon ! for Somebody !
    Oh-hey ! for Somebody !
I wad do—what wad I not ?
For the sake o' Somebody !

O MAY, THY MORN.

O MAY, thy morn was ne'er sae sweet,
    As the mirk night o' December;
For sparkling was the rosy wine,
    And private was the chamber:
And dear was she I dare na name,
    But I will aye remember.
        And dear, etc.

And here's to them, that, like oursel,
    Can push about the jorum,
And here's to them that wish us weel,
    May a' that's guid watch o'er them;
And here's to them we dare na tell,
    The dearest o' the quorum.
        And here's to, etc.

THE LOVELY LASS OF INVERNESS.

THE lovely lass o' Inverness,
    Nae joy nor pleasure can she see;
For e'en and morn she cries, Alas!
    And aye the saut tear blins her ee:—
Drumossie moor, Drumossie day,
    A waefu' day it was to me;
For there I lost my father dear,
    My father dear and brethren three.

Their winding-sheet the bluidy clay,
    Their graves are growing green to see;
And by them lies the dearest lad
    That ever blest a woman's e'e!
Now wae to thee thou cruel lord,
    A bluidy man I trow thou be;
For mony a heart thou hast made sair,
    That ne'er did wrang to thine or thee!

A RED, RED ROSE.

TUNE—"*Wishaw's favourite.*"

O, MY Luve's like a red, red rose
   That's newly sprung in June;
O, my Luve's like the melodie
   That's sweetly play'd in tune.

As fair art thou, my bonie lass,
   So deep in luve am I:
And I will luve thee still, my Dear,
   Till a' the seas gang dry.

Till a' the seas gang dry, my Dear,
   And the rocks melt wi' the sun:
And I will luve thee still, my Dear,
   While the sands o' life shall run.

And fare thee weel, my only Luve!
   And fare thee weel, awhile!
And I will come again, my Luve,
   Tho' it ware ten thousand mile!

ADDRESS TO A LADY.

OH wert thou in the cauld blast,
   On yonder lea, on yonder lea,
My plaidie to the angry airt,
   I'd shelter thee, I'd shelter thee:
Or did misfortune's bitter storms
   Around thee blaw, around thee blaw,
Thy beild should be my bosom,
   To share it a' to share it a'.

Or were I in the wildest waste,
   Sae black and bare, sae black and bare,
The desart were a paradise,
   If thou wert there, if thou wert there.
Or were I Monarch o' the globe,
   Wi' thee to reign, wi' thee to reign,
The brightest jewel in my crown
   Wad be my Queen, wad be my Queen.

UP IN THE MORNING EARLY.

CAULD blaws the wind frae east to west,
    The drift is driving sairly;
Sae loud and shrill's I hear the blast,—
    I'm sure it's winter fairly.

       CHORUS.
  Up in the morning's no for me,
    Up in the morning early;
  When a' the hills are cover'd wi' snaw,
    I'm sure it's winter fairly.

The birds sit chittering in the thorn,
    A' day they fare but sparely;
And lang's the night frae e'en to morn—
    I'm sure it's winter fairly.
    Up in the morning's no for me,
      Up in the morning early;
    When a' the hills are cover'd wi' snaw,
      I'm sure it's winter fairly.

MY BONIE MARY.

Go fetch to me a pint o' wine,
    And fill it in a silver tassie;
That I may drink before I go
    A service to my bonie lassie.
The boat rocks at the Pier o' Leith;
    Fu' loud the wind blaws frae the Ferry;
The ship rides by the Berwick-law,
    And I maun leave my bonie Mary.

The trumpets sound, the banners fly,
    The glittering spears are ranked ready;
The shouts o' war are heard afar,
    The battle closes deep and bloody;
It's not the roar o' sea or shore
    Wad mak me langer wish to tarry;
Nor shouts o' war that's heard afar,
    It's leaving thee, my bonie Mary.

MY HEART'S IN THE HIGHLANDS.

MY heart's in the Highlands, my heart is not here;
My heart's in the Highlands a-chasing the deer;
A-chasing the wild deer, and following the roe,
My heart's in the Highlands wherever I go.
Farewell to the Highlands, farewell to the North,
The birthplace of Valour, the country of Worth;
Wherever I wander, wherever I rove,
The hills of the Highlands for ever I love.

Farewell to the mountains high-cover'd with snow;
Farewell to the straths and green valleys below:
Farewell to the forests and wild-hanging woods;
Farewell to the torrents and loud-pouring floods.
My heart's in the Highlands, my heart is not here,
My heart's in the Highlands a-chasing the deer:
A-chasing the wild deer, and following the roe;
My heart's in the Highlands wherever I go.

THERE'S A YOUTH IN THIS CITY.

A Galic Air.

THERE'S a youth in this city, it were a great pity
    That he from our lasses should wander awa;
For he's bonie and braw, weel favour'd witha',
    And his hair has a natural buckle and a'.
His coat is the hue o' his bonnet sae blue;
    His fecket is white as the new-driven snaw;
His hose they are blae, and his shoon like the slae,
    And his clear siller buckles they dazzle us a'.
        His coat is the hue, etc.

For beauty and fortune the laddie's been courtin;
    Weel-featur'd, weel-tocher'd, weel-mounted and braw;
But chiefly the siller, that gars him gang till her,
    The Pennie's the jewel that beautifies a'.
There's Meg wi' the mailin that fain wad a haen him,
    And Susy, whase daddy was Laird o' the Ha';
There's lang-tocher'd Nancy maist fetters his fancy—
    But the laddie's dear sel he lo'es dearest of a'.

AE FOND KISS.

AE fond kiss, and then we sever;
Ae fareweel, and then for ever!
Deep in heart-wrung tears I'll pledge thee,
Warring sighs and groans I'll wage thee.
Who shall say that fortune grieves him
While the star of hope she leaves him?
Me, nae cheerfu' twinkle lights me,
Dark despair around benights me.

I'll ne'er blame my partial fancy,
Naething could resist my Nancy:
But to see her was to love her;
Love but her, and love for ever.
Had we never lov'd sae kindly.
Had we never lov'd sae blindly,
Never met—or never parted,
We had ne'er been broken-hearted.

Fare thee weel, thou first and fairest!
Fare thee weel, thou best and dearest!
Thine be ilka joy and treasure,
Peace, Enjoyment, Love and Pleasure!

Ae fond kiss, and then we sever;
Ae fareweel, Alas! for ever!
Deep in heart-wrung tears I'll pledge thee,
Warring sighs and groans I'll wage thee.

OUT OVER THE FORTH.

OUT over the Forth, I look to the North;
    But what is the North and its Highlands to me?
The South nor the East gie ease to my breast,
    The far foreign land, or the wild rolling sea.

But I look to the West when I gae to rest,
    That happy my dreams and my slumbers may be;
For far in the West lives he I loe best,
    The man that is dear to my babie and me.

JOHN BARLEYCORN.

A BALLAD.

THERE was three kings into the east,
    Three kings both great and high,
And they hae sworn a solemn oath
    John Barleycorn should die.

They took a plough and plough'd him down,
    Put clods upon his head,
And they hae sworn a solemn oath
    John Barleycorn was dead.

But the cheerfu' Spring came kindly on,
    And show'rs began to fall;
John Barleycorn got up again,
    And sore surpris'd them all.

The sultry suns of Summer came,
    And he grew thick and strong,
His head weel arm'd wi' pointed spears,
    That no one should him wrong.

The sober Autumn enter'd mild,
    When he grew wan and pale;
His bending joints and drooping head
    Show'd he began to fail.

His colour sicken'd more and more,
    He faded into age;
And then his enemies began
    To show their deadly rage.

They've taen a weapon, long and sharp,
    And cut him by the knee;
Then tied him fast upon a cart,
    Like a rogue for forgerie.

They laid him down upon his back,
    And cudgell'd him full sore;
They hung him up before the storm,
    And turn'd him o'er and o'er.

They filled up a darksome pit
    With water to the brim,
They heaved in John Barleycorn,
    There let him sink or swim.

They laid him out upon the floor,
    To work him farther woe,

And still, as signs of life appear'd,
    They toss'd him to and fro.

They wasted, o'er a scorching flame,
    The marrow of his bones;
But a Miller us'd him worst of all,
    For he crush'd him between two stones.

And they hae taen his very heart's blood,
    And drank it round and round;
And still the more and more they drank,
    Their joy did more abound.

John Barleycorn was a hero bold,
    Of noble enterprise;
For if you do but taste his blood,
    'Twill make your courage rise.

'Twill make a man forget his woe;
    'Twill heighten all his joy:
'Twill make the widow's heart to sing,
    Tho' the tear were in her eye.

Then let us toast John Barleycorn,
    Each man a glass in hand;
And may his great posterity
    Ne'er fail in old Scotland!

THE RIGS O' BARLEY.

Tune—"*Corn rigs are bonie.*"

I.

IT was upon a Lammas night,
    When corn rigs are bonie,
Beneath the moon's unclouded light,
    I held awa to Annie:
The time flew by, wi' tentless head,
    Till, 'tween the late and early,
Wi' sma' persuasion she agreed,
    To see me thro' the barley.

II.

The sky was blue, the wind was still,
    The moon was shining clearly;
I set her down, wi' right good will,
    Amang the rigs o' barley:
I ken't her heart was a' my ain;
    I lov'd her most sincerely;
I kiss'd her owre and owre again,
    Amang the rigs o' barley.

III.

I lock'd her in my fond embrace;
    Her heart was beating rarely:
My blessings on that happy place,
    Amang the rigs o' barley!
But by the moon and stars so bright,
    That shone that hour so clearly!
She ay shall bless that happy night
    Amang the rigs o' barley.

IV.

I hae been blythe wi' Comrades dear;
    I hae been merry drinking;
I hae been joyfu' gath'rin gear;
    I hae been happy thinking:
But a' the pleasures e'er I saw,
    Tho' three times doubl'd fairly,
That happy night was worth them a',
    Amang the rigs o' barley.

CHORUS.

Corn rigs, an' barley rigs,
    An' corn rigs are bonie:
I'll ne'er forget that happy night,
    Amang the rigs wi' Annie.

SONG.

Tune—"*My Nanie, O.*"

BEHIND yon hills where Stinchar flows,
   'Mang moors an' mosses many, O,
The wintry sun the day has clos'd,
   And I'll awa' to Nanie, O.

The westlin wind blaws loud an' shill;
   The night's baith mirk and rainy, O:
But I'll get my plaid an' out I'll steal,
   An' owre the hill to Nanie, O.

My Nanie's charming, sweet an' young;
   Nae artfu' wiles to win ye, O:
May ill befa' the flattering tongue
   That wad beguile my Nanie, O.

Her face is fair, her heart is true;
   As spotless as she's bonie, O;
The op'ning gowan, wat wi' dew,
   Nae purer is than Nanie, O.

A country lad is my degree,
  An' few there be that ken me, O ;
But what care I how few they be,
  I'm welcome ay to Nanie, O.

My riches a's my penny-fee,
  An' I maun guide it cannie, O ;
But warl's gear ne'er troubles me,
  My thoughts are a'—my Nanie, O.

Our auld Guidman delights to view
  His sheep an' kye thrive bonie, O ;
But I'm as blythe that hauds his pleugh,
  An' has nae care but Nanie, O.

Come weel, come woe, I care na by,
  I'll tak what Heav'n will send me, O :
Nae ither care in life have I,
  But live, an' love my Nanie, O.

GREEN GROW THE RASHES.

A FRAGMENT.

CHORUS. Green grow the rashes, O ;
          Green grow the rashes, O ;
          The sweetest hours that e'er I spend,
          Are spent amang the lasses, O.

I.

THERE'S nought but care on ev'ry han',
    In ev'ry hour that passes, O :
What signifies the life o' man,
    An' 'twere na for the lasses, O.
        Green grow, etc.

II.

The warly race may riches chase,
    An' riches still may fly them, O ;
An' tho' at last they catch them fast,
    Their hearts can ne'er enjoy them, O.
        Green grow, etc.

III.

But gie me a canny hour at e'en,
    My arms about my Dearie, O ;
An' warly cares, an' warly men,
    May a' gae tapsalteerie, O !
        Green grow, etc.

IV.

For you sae douse, ye sneer at this,
    Ye're nought but senseless asses, O :
The wisest Man the warl' saw,
    He dearly lov'd the lasses, O.
        Green grow, etc.

V.

Auld Nature swears, the lovely Dears
    Her noblest work she classes, O ;
Her prentice han' she try'd on man,
    An' then she made the lasses, O.
        Green grow, etc.

*   *   *   *

YE BANKS, AND BRAES, AND STREAMS AROUND.

TUNE—"*Katharine Ogie.*"

YE banks, and braes, and streams around
    The castle of Montgomery,
Green be your woods, and fair your flowers,
    Your waters never drumlie!
There simmer first unfauld her robes,
    And there the langest tarry:
For there I took the last farewell
    O' my sweet Highland Mary.

How sweetly bloom'd the gay, green birk,
    How rich the hawthorn's blossom;
As underneath their fragrant shade,
    I clasp'd her to my bosom!
The golden Hours, on angel wings
    Flew o'er me and my Dearie;
For dear to me as light and life,
    Was my sweet Highland Mary.

Wi' mony a vow, and lock'd embrace,
    Our parting was fu' tender;

And, pledging aft to meet again,
  We tore oursels asunder.
But oh! fell Death's untimely frost,
  That nipt my Flower sae early!
Now green's the sod, and cauld's the clay,
  That wraps my Highland Mary!

O pale, pale now, those rosy lips
  I aft hae kiss'd sae fondly!
And closed for ay, the sparkling glance
    That dwalt on me sae kindly!
And mouldering now in silent dust,
  That heart that lo'ed me dearly!
But still within my bosom's core
  Shall live my Highland Mary.

AULD LANG SYNE.

SHOULD auld acquaintance be forgot,
  And never brought to min'?
Should auld acquaintance be forgot,
  And auld lang syne?

CHORUS.

For auld lang syne my dear,
  For auld lang syne,
We'll tak a cup o' kindness yet,
  For auld lang syne.

And surely ye'll be your pint-stowp!
  And surely I'll be mine!
And we'll tak a cup o' kindness yet,
  For auld lang syne.
    For auld, etc.

We twa hae run about the braes,
  And pou'd the gowans fine;
But we've wander'd mony a weary fitt
  Sin' auld lang syne.
    For auld, etc.

We twa hae paidlet i' the burn,
  Fra' morning sun till dine;
But seas between us braid hae roar'd
  Sin' auld lang syne.
    For auld, etc.

And there's a hand, my trusty fiere!
  And gie's a hand o' thine!
And we'll tak a right gude-willie waught,
  For auld lang syne.
    For auld, etc.

BRUCE'S ADDRESS TO HIS ARMY AT BANNOCKBURN.

TUNE—"*Hey tuttie tattie.*"

SCOTS, wha hae wi' Wallace bled !
Scots, wham Bruce has aften led !
Welcome to your gory bed,
　Or to glorious Victorie !

Now's the day, and now's the hour ;
See the front o' battle lour ;
See approach proud Edward's power,—
　Edward, Chains and Slavery !

Wha will be a traitor knave ?
Wha can fill a coward's grave ?
Wha sae base as be a Slave ?
　Traitor, Coward, turn and flee !

Wha for Scotland's King and Law,
Freedom's sword will strongly draw ;
Free-man stand, or Free-man fa',
　Caledonian, on wi' me.

By oppression's woes and pains !
By your Sons in servile chains !
We will drain our dearest veins,
   But they shall be SHALL be Free !

Lay the proud Usurpers low !
Tyrants fall in every foe !
Liberty's in every blow !
   Forward,—let us Do—or Die ! ! !

So may God ever defend the cause of Truth and Liberty, as he did that day ! Amen !—R. B.

FOR A' THAT AND A' THAT.

IS there, for honest poverty
   That hangs his head, an' a' that ;
The coward-slave, we pass him by,
   We dare be poor for a' that !
     For a' that, an' a' that,
       Our toils obscure and a' that,
       The rank is but a guinea's stamp ;
       The Man's the gowd for a' that.

What though on hamely fare we dine,
   Wear hoddin grey, an' a' that ;
Gie fools their silks, and knaves their wine,
   A Man's a Man for a' that :

    For a' that, an' a' that,
      Their tinsel show, an' a' that;
    The honest man, though e'er sae poor,
      Is king o' men for a' that.

Ye see yon birkie, ca'd a lord,
  Wha struts, and stares, an' a' that;
Tho' hundreds worship at his word,
  He's but a coof for a' that:
    For a' that, an' a' that,
      His ribband, star, an' a' that,
    The man o' independent mind,
      He looks an' laughs at a' that.

A prince can mak a belted knight,
  A marquis, duke, an' a' that;
But an honest man's aboon his might,
  Guid faith he mauna fa' that!
    For a' that, an' a' that,
      Their dignities, an' a' that,
    The pith o' sense, and pride o' worth,
      Are higher rank than a' that.

Then let us pray that come it may,
  (As come it will for a' that,)
That Sense and Worth, o'er a' the earth,
  Should bear the gree, an' a' that

For a' that and a' that,
It's comin yet for a' that,
That man to man, the warld o'er,
Shall brothers be for a' that.

THE DUMFRIES VOLUNTEERS.

TUNE—"*Push about the jorum.*"

April, 1795.

DOES haughty Gaul invasion threat?
   Then let the loons beware, sir,
There's Wooden Walls upon our seas,
   And Volunteers on shore, sir.
The Nith shall run to Corsincon,[1]
   And Criffel[2] sink to Solway,
Ere we permit a foreign foe
   On British ground to rally !
          Fall de rall, etc.

O let us not like snarling tykes
   In wrangling be divided ;
Till, slap ! come in an unco loon
   And wi' a rung decide it.

---

[1] Corsincon, a high hill at the source of the river Nith.
[2] Criffel, a mountain at the mouth of the same river.

Be Britain still to Britain true,
   Amang oursels united;
For never but by British hands
   Maun British wrangs be righted!
                Fall de rall, etc.

The kettle o' the kirk and state,
   Perhaps a claut may fail in't;
But deil a foreign tinkler loon
   Shall ever ca' a nail in't.
Our fathers' bluid the kettle bought,
   And wha wad dare to spoil it;
By Heav'ns! the sacrilegious dog
   Shall fuel be to boil it!
                Fall de rall, etc.

The wretch that wad a tyrant own,
   And the wretch his true-born brother,
Who would set the Mob aboon the Throne,
   May they be damned together!
Who will not sing "God save the King,"
   Shall hang as high's the steeple;
But while we sing, "God save the King,"
   We'll ne'er forget the people.

MARY MORISON.

Tune—"*Bide ye yet.*"

O MARY, at thy window be,
   It is the wish'd, the trysted hour!
Those smiles and glances let me see,
   That make the miser's treasure poor:
How blythely wad I bide the stoure,
   A weary slave frae sun to sun;
Could I the rich reward secure,
   The lovely Mary Morison.

Yestreen, when to the trembling string
   The dance gaed thro' the lighted ha',
To thee my fancy took its wing,
   I sat, but neither heard nor saw:
Tho' this was fair, and that was braw,
   And yon the toast of a' the town,
I sigh'd, and said amang them a',
   "Ye are na Mary Morison."

O Mary, canst thou wreck his peace,
   Wha for thy sake wad gladly die?
Or canst thou break that heart of his,
   Whase only faut is loving thee?

If love for love thou wilt na gie,
   At least be pity to me shown ;
A thought ungentle canna be
   The thought o' Mary Morison.

O SAW YE BONIE LESLEY.

TUNE—"*The Collier's bonie Lassie.*"

O SAW ye bonie Lesley,
   As she gaed o'er the border?
She's gane, like Alexander,
   To spread her conquests farther.
To see her, is to love her,
   And love but her for ever ;
For Nature made her what she is,
   And never made anither !

Thou art a queen, fair Lesley,
   Thy subjects we before thee :
Thou art divine, fair Lesley,
   The hearts of men adore thee.
The Deil he cou'dna scaith thee,
   Or aught that wad belang thee !
He'd look into thy bonie face,
   And say, " I canna wrang thee."

The Powers aboon will tent thee,
  Misfortune sha'na steer thee ;
Thou'rt like themsels sae lovely,
  That ill they'll ne'er let near thee.
Return again, fair Lesley,
  Return to Caledonie !
That we may brag we hae a lass
  There's nane again sae bonie.

WOMEN'S MINDS.

Tune—"*For a' that.*"

THO' women's minds, like winter winds
  May shift and turn, and a' that,
The noblest breast adores them maist,—
  A consequence I draw that.

  For a' that, an' a' that,
    And twice as meikle's a' that,
  The bonie lass that I loe best
    She'll be my ain for a' that.

Great love I bear to all the fair,
  Their humble slave, and a' that ;

But lordly will, I hold it still
   A mortal sin to thraw that.
      For a' that, etc.

But there is ane aboon the lave,
   Has wit, and sense, and a' that;
A bonie lass, I like her best,
   And wha a crime dare ca' that?
      For a' that, etc.

In rapture sweet this hour we meet,
   Wi' mutual love, an' a' that;
But for how lang the flie may stang,
   Let inclination law that.
      For a' that, etc.

Their tricks an' craft hae put me daft,
   They've ta'en me in, an' a' that;
But clear your decks, and—here's "The Sex!"
   I like the jades for a' that.
      For a' that, etc.

TO MARY IN HEAVEN.

TUNE—"*Miss Forbes' farewell to Banff.*"

THOU lingering star, with less'ning ray,
    That lov'st to greet the early morn,
Again thou usher'st in the day
    My Mary from my soul was torn.
O Mary! dear departed shade!
    Where is thy place of blissful rest?
Seest thou thy lover lowly laid?
    Hear'st thou the groans that rend his breast?

That sacred hour can I forget?
    Can I forget the hallow'd grove,
Where, by the winding Ayr, we met,
    To live one day of parting love?
Eternity will not efface
    Those records dear of transports past;
Thy image at our last embrace,—
    Ah! little thought we 'twas our last!

Ayr, gurgling kiss'd his pebbled shore,
    O'erhung with wild-woods, thick'ning green;
The fragrant birch, and hawthorn hoar,
    Twin'd am'rous round the raptur'd scene:

The flowers sprang wanton to be prest,
    The birds sang love on ev'ry spray,
Till too, too soon, the glowing west
    Proclaim'd the speed of winged day.

Still o'er these scenes my mem'ry wakes,
    And fondly broods with miser-care!
Time but the impression stronger makes,
    As streams their channels deeper wear.
My Mary! dear departed shade!
    Where is thy place of blissful rest?
Seest thou thy lover lowly laid?
    Hear'st thou the groans that rend his breast?

PATRIOTIC SONG.

HERE'S a health to them that's awa,
Here's a health to them that's awa;
And wha winna wish guid luck to our cause,
May never guid luck be their fa'!
It's guid to be merry and wise,
It's guid to be honest and true,
It's guid to support Caledonia's cause,
And bide by the buff and the blue.

Here's a health to them that's awa,
Here's a health to them that's awa,
Here's a health to Charlie the chief o' the clan,
Altho' that his band be sma'.
May Liberty meet wi' success!
May Prudence protect her frae evil!
May tyrants and tyranny tine i' the mist,
And wander their way to the devil!

Here's a health to them that's awa,
Here's a health to them that's awa,
Here's a health to Tammie, the Norland laddie,
That lives at the lug o' the law!
Here's freedom to him that wad read,
Here's freedom to him that wad write!
There's nane ever fear'd that the truth should be heard,
But they wham the truth wad indite.

Here's a health to them that's awa,
Here's a health to them that's awa,
Here's Chieftain M'Leod, a Chieftain worth gowd,
Tho' bred among mountains o' snaw!

* * * * *

AWA WHIGS, AWA.

CHORUS.   Awa Whigs, awa!
         Awa Whigs, awa!
    Ye're but a pack o' traitor louns,
      Ye'll do nae good at a'.

OUR thrissles flourish'd fresh and fair,
    And bonie bloom'd our roses;
But Whigs came like a frost in June,
    And wither'd a' our posies.

    Awa Whigs, awa!
    Awa Whigs, awa!
Ye're but a pack o' traitor louns,
    Ye'll do nae good at a'.

Our ancient crown's fa'en in the dust;
    Deil blin' them wi' the stoure o't!
And write their names in his black beuk,
    Wha gae the Whigs the power o't.
          Awa Whigs, etc.

Our sad decay in church and state
    Surpasses my descriving:

The Whigs cam o'er us for a curse,
   And we hae done wi' thriving.
                Awa Whigs, etc.

Grim Vengeance lang has ta'en a nap,
   But we may see him wauken:
Gude help the day when Royal heads
   Are hunted like a mauken!

    Awa Whigs, awa!
    Awa Whigs, awa!
Ye're but a pack o' traitor louns,
   Ye'll do nae gude at a'.

BRAW LADS OF GALLA WATER.

TUNE—"*Galla Water.*"

CHORUS. Braw, braw lads of Galla Water;
       O braw lads of Galla Water:
      I'll kilt my coats aboon my knee,
       And follow my love through the water.

SAE fair her hair, sae brent her brow,
   Sae bonie blue her een, my dearie;
Sae white her teeth, sae sweet her mou',
   The mair I kiss she's ay my dearie.

O'er yon bank and o'er yon brae,
  O'er yon moss amang the heather;
I'll kilt my coats aboon my knee,
  And follow my love through the water.

Down amang the broom, the broom,
  Down amang the broom, my dearie,
The lassie lost a silken snood,
  That cost her mony a blirt and bleary.
    Braw, braw lads of Galla Water;
    O braw lads of Galla Water:
    I'll kilt my coats aboon my knee,
      And follow my love through the water.

COMING THROUGH THE RYE.

Tune—"Coming through the rye."

COMING through the rye, poor body,
  Coming through the rye,
She draiglet a' her petticoatie,
  Coming through the rye.
Jenny's a' wat, poor body,
  Jenny's seldom dry;
She draiglet a' her petticoatie,
  Coming through the rye.

Gin a body meet a body—
   Coming through the rye ;
Gin a body kiss a body—
   Need a body cry ?

Gin a body meet a body
   Coming through the glen,
Gin a body kiss a body—
   Need the world ken ?
Jenny's a' wat, poor body ;
   Jenny's seldom dry ;
She draiglet a' her petticoatie,
   Coming through the rye.

HEY, THE DUSTY MILLER.

TUNE—"*The Dusty Miller.*"

HEY, the Dusty Miller,
   And his dusty coat;
He will win a shilling,
   Or he spend a groat.
   Dusty was the coat,
      Dusty was the colour,
   Dusty was the kiss
      That I got frae the Miller.

Hey, the dusty Miller,
  And his dusty sack;
Leeze me on the calling
  Fills the dusty peck:
    Fills the dusty peck,
      Brings the dusty siller;
    I wad gie my coatie
      For the dusty Miller.

THE CARDIN' O'T.

TUNE—"*Salt Fish and Dumplings.*"

I COFT a stane o' haslock woo',
  To make a wab to Johnie o't;
For Johnie is my only jo,
  I lo'e him best of onie yet.
    The cardin' o't, the spinnin' o't,
      The warpin' o't, the winnin' o't;
    When ilka ell cost me a groat,
      The taylor staw the lynin o't.

For though his locks be lyart gray,
  And though his brow be beld aboon,
Yet I hae seen him on a day
  The pride of a' the parishen.

The cardin' o't, the spinnin' o't,
    The warpin' o't, the winnin' o't;
When ilka ell cost me a groat,
    The tailor staw the lynin o't.

IT WAS A' FOR OUR RIGHTFU' KING.

IT was a' for our rightfu' king
    We left fair Scotland's strand;
It was a' for our rightfu' king
    We e'er saw Irish land
        My dear,
We e'er saw Irish land.

Now a' is done that men can do,
    And a' is done in vain:
My Love and Native Land farewell,
    For I maun cross the main,
        My dear,
For I maun cross the main.

He turn'd him right and round about,
    Upon the Irish shore;
And gae his bridle-reins a shake,

With adieu for evermore,
        My dear,
With adieu for evermore.

The soger frae the wars returns,
  The sailor frae the main ;
But I hae parted frae my Love,
  Never to meet again,
        My dear,
Never to meet again.

When day is gane, and night is come,
  And a' folk bound to sleep ;
I think on him that's far awa',
  The lee-lang night and weep,
        My dear,
The lee-lang night, and weep.

O KENMURE'S ON AND AWA, WILLIE.

TUNE—"*O Kenmure's on and awa, Willie.*"

O KENMURE'S on and awa, Willie,
  O Kenmure's on and awa ;
An' Kenmure's Lord's the bravest Lord
  That ever Galloway saw.

Success to Kenmure's band, Willie !
　Success to Kenmure's band !
There's no a heart that fears a Whig
　That rides by Kenmure's hand.

Here's Kenmure's health in wine, Willie !
　Here's Kenmure's health in wine !
There ne'er was a coward o' Kenmure's blude,
　Nor yet o' Gordon's Line.

O Kenmure's lads are men, Willie,
　O Kenmure's lads are men ;
Their hearts and swords are metal true,
　And that their faes shall ken.

They'll live, or die wi' fame, Willie,
　They'll live or die wi' fame ;
But soon, wi' sounding Victorie,
　May Kenmure's Lord come hame !

Here's Him that's far awa, Willie !
　Here's Him that's far awa !
And here's the flower that I loe best,
　The rose that's like the snaw.

SIMMER'S A PLEASANT TIME.

Tune—"*Ay waukin, O.*"

SIMMER'S a pleasant time,
   Flow'rs of ev'ry colour;
The water rins o'er the heugh,
   And I long for my true lover!
     Ay waukin O,
       Waukin still and weary:
     Sleep I can get nane
       For thinking on my Dearie.

When I sleep I dream,
   When I wauk I'm eerie;
Sleep I can get nane
   For thinking on my Dearie.

Lanely night comes on,
   A' the lave are sleepin;
I think on my bonie lad
   And I bleer my een with greetin'.
     Ay waukin O,
       Waukin still and weary;
     Sleep I can get nane
       For thinking on my Dearie.

THE HIGHLAND LADDIE.

TUNE—"*If thou'lt play me fair play.*"

THE boniest lad that e'er I saw,
　　Bonie laddie, Highland laddie,
Wore a plaid and was fu' braw,
　　Bonie Highland laddie.
On his head a bonnet blue,
　　Bonie laddie, Highland laddie,
His royal heart was firm and true,
　　Bonie Highland laddie.

Trumpets sound and cannons roar,
　　Bonie lassie, Lawland lassie,
And a' the hills wi' echoes roar,
　　Bonie Lawland lassie.
Glory, Honour, now invite,
　　Bonie lassie, Lawland lassie,
For Freedom and my King to fight,
　　Bonie Lawland lassie.

The sun a backward course shall take,
　　Bonie laddie, Highland laddie,
Ere aught thy manly courage shake;
　　Bonie Highland laddie.

Go, for yoursel procure renown,
  Bonie laddie, Highland laddie,
And for your lawful King his crown,
  Bonie Highland laddie!

WEARY FA' YOU, DUNCAN GRAY.

TUNE—"*Duncan Gray.*"

WEARY fa' you, Duncan Gray—
  Ha, ha, the girdin o't!
Wae gae by you, Duncan Gray—
  Ha, ha, the girdin o't!
When a' the lave gae to their play,
Then I maun sit the lee-lang day,
And jog the cradle wi' my tae,
  And a' for the girdin o't.

Bonnie was the Lammas moon—
  Ha, ha, the girdin o't!
Glowrin' a' the hills aboon—
  Ha, ha, the girdin o't!
The girdin brak, the beast cam down,
I tint my curch, and baith my shoon
Ah! Duncan, ye're an unco loon—
  Wae on the bad girdin o't!

But, Duncan, gin ye'll keep your aith—
   Ha, ha, the girdin o't !
Ise bless you wi' my hindmost breath—
   Ha, ha, the girdin o't !
Duncan, gin ye'll keep your aith,
The beast again can bear us baith,
And auld Mess John will mend the skaith,
   And clout the bad girdin o't.

YE JACOBITES BY NAME.

TUNE—"*Ye Jacobites by name.*"

YE Jacobites by name, give an ear, give an ear ;
   Ye Jacobites by name, give an ear ;
Ye Jacobites by name,
   Your fautes I will proclaim,
Your doctrines I maun blame,
     You shall hear.

What is Right and what is Wrang, by the law, by the law ?
What is Right and what is Wrang by the law ?
   What is Right and what is Wrang ?
   A short sword, and a lang,
A weak arm, and a strang
     For to draw.

What makes heroic strife, fam'd a far, fam'd a far?
What makes heroic strife fam'd afar?
    What makes heroic strife?
    To whet th' assassin's knife,
Or hunt a Parent's life
        Wi' bludie war?

Then let your schemes alone, in the state, in the state;
Then let your schemes alone, in the state;
    Then let your schemes alone,
    Adore the rising sun,
And leave a man undone
        To his fate.

WHAN I SLEEP I DREAM.

WHAN I sleep I dream,
    Whan I wauk I'm eerie,
Sleep I canna get,
    For thinkin' o' my dearie.

Lanely night comes on,
    A' the house are sleeping,
I think on the bonie lad
    That has my heart a keeping.

Ay waukin O, waukin ay and wearie,
Sleep I canna get, for thinkin' o' my dearie,

Lanely night comes on,
  A' the house are sleeping,
I think on my bonie lad,
  An' I bleer my een wi' greetin'!
    Ay waukin, etc.

WHEN I THINK ON THE HAPPY DAYS.

WHEN I think on the happy days
  I spent wi' you, my dearie;
And now what lands between us lie,
  How can I be but eerie!

How slow ye move, ye heavy hours,
  As ye were wae and weary!
It was na sae ye glinten by
  When I was wi' my dearie.

GLOSSARY.

GLOSSARY.

Abeigh, at a shy distance.
Ae, one.
Aiblins, perhaps.
Airn, iron.
Airt, quarter of the compass.
Aizle, a hot cinder.
A-kennin, knowingly.
Ase, wood ashes.
Asklent, aslant.
Asteer, abroad, astir.
Aumos, alms.
Awnie, bearded.

Backet, bucket.
Bairn-time, a brood of children.
Barley-brie, barley-brew; beer.
Bauckie, a bat.
Bauk, a cross beam.
Baws'nt, having a white stripe down the face.
Bear, barley.
Beets, boots.
Beild, a shelter.
Belyve, presently.
Ben, within, the room within, or parlour.

Bicker, a wooden dish.
Biggin, building.
Billies, young fellows.
Bing, a heap.
Birk, birch.
Birken, of birch.
Birken-shaw, wood of birch.
Birkie, a clever fellow.
Blate, bashful.
Bleary, with wet eyes; blirt and bleary=outburst of grief with tears.
Bleeze, to blaze.
Bleezing, blazing.
Blellum, an idle chatterer.
Blethering, an idle talker.
Blethers, foolish talk.
Blinker, a term of contempt.
Blirt, outburst of grief.
Blue-clue, a ball of blue worsted.
Bluntie, a stupid person.
Blype, a shred.
Boddle, a small copper coin.
Bogle, a ghost.
Boortrie, an elder-bush.
Bore, a cranny.

Bow-kail, cabbage.
Brae, a hill slope.
Braing, to plunge, or fret.
Brash, a sudden illness.
Brattle, a short race.
Braw, fine.
Brawlie, finely.
Braxie, a diseased sheep.
Breckan, bracken.
Bree, brew.
Brent, bright.
Brisket, breast.
Brogue, a trick.
Broo, broth.
Broose, broth.
Brugh, a burgh, town.
Brulzie, a broil.
Brunt, burnt.
Buckskin, a Virginian.
Bughtin-time, the time for folding sheep.
Buirdly, stoutly made.
Bum-clock, a cockchafer.
Bure, bore, past tense of bear.
Burn, a small stream.
Busk, to dress.
But and ben, without and within = the kitchen and parlour.
Byke, a bee-hive.

Caddie, a young fellow.
Caird, a tinker.
Callan, a boy.
Callet, a whore.
Caller, or *callor*, fresh.
Cannie, crafty.
Canny, gentle.
Cantie, cheerful.
Cantraip, a charm or spell.
Cant, to tell merry tales.
Carlin, an old woman.
Cauk, chalk.
Causey, causeway.
Cavie, a hencoop.
Chield, child.
Chiel, child.
Chuck, a hen = a woman.
Claut, a heap.
Cleading, clothing.
Cleed, to clothe.
Cleek, to hook.
Clishmaclaver, idle talk.
Clockin' time, hatching time.
Clootie, hoofed one; a name for the devil.
Clour, a lump.
Coble, a boat.
Coft, bought.
Cog, coggie, a wooden dish.
Cood, the cud.
Coof, a blockhead.
Coost, cast.
Cootie, a small tub.
Core, a corps.
Corn't, to feed with oats.
Couthy, kind.
Cowe, a set down.
Crabbet, fretful.
Crack, to talk.
Crack, a chat.
Craig, craigie, the neck, or throat.
Cranreuch, hoar-frost.

GLOSSARY. 217

Creel, a basket; to have one's senses in a creel = to be confused.
Creeshie, greasy.
Croon, to hum.
Croose, crouse, cheerful.
Crouchie, crook-backed.
Crowdie, porridge; crowdie-time = breakfast time.
Crummock, a cow with crooked horns.
Crump, crisp.
Crunt, a blow on the head.
Curpan, the crupper.
Cushat, the wood-pigeon.
Custocks, the pith of a cabbage stalk.
Cutty, short.

Daffin, foolish merriment.
Daft, foolish.
Dail, a plank.
Daurk, a day's labour.
Dawd, a large piece.
Dawted, petted.
Deave, to deafen.
Deil, the devil.
Dight, to wipe, or clean.
Ding, to beat, surpass.
Donsie, unlucky.
Dool, sorrow.
Douce, wise.
Doure, sullen,
Douse, wise.
Dowf, weakly.
Dowie, worn out with fatigue.

Doylt, stupefied.
Dreigh, to endure.
Drouthy, thirsty.
Drumly, muddy.
Drunt, ill-humour.
Driddle, to move slowly.
Drift, fell aff the drift = wandered away from the company.
Dub, a puddle.
Duddie, ragged.
Duds, duddies, rags.
Dusht, pushed by an ox = dazed.

Eerie, haunted.
Eldritch, elvish.
Ettle, aim, attempt.
Eydent, diligent.

Fa', he mauna fa' that = have that as his lot.
Faddom't, measured.
Fain, glad.
Farl, an oat-cake.
Fash, to care for.
Fauld, to fold.
Fause-house, an empty space in a corn-stack.
Fawsont, seemly.
Feat, neat.
Fecht, to fight.
Feck, plenty.
Fecket, a sleeved waistcoat.
Fell, sharp and biting.
Fen', defend.
Ferlie, wonder.

GLOSSARY.

Fidge, to fidget.
Fiel, soft.
Fiere, a friend.
Fitt, a foot.
Fittie-lan', the near wheeler of a team.
Fleech, to supplicate in a flattering manner.
Fley, to scare.
Flichter, to flitter.
Flingin-tree, a flail.
Flisket, fretted.
Fodgel, short and fat.
Forbye, besides.
Fou, full = drunk.
Fouth, enough.
Fud, the scut of a hare or rabbit.
Fyke, trifling annoyance.
Fyle, to soil.

Gab, the mouth = conversation
Gangrel, a wanderer.
Gar, to cause, to make.
Gart, caused.
Gash, wise.
Gashan, talking.
Gate, way.
Gaucie, gausy, gawcie, large.
Gear, riches, or goods.
Geordie, a guinea.
Gilpey, half-grown.
Girdle, or *griddle*, an iron plate for baking cakes.
Girn, to grin.
Gizz, a wig.
Glaikit, foolish.

Glaizie, glittering.
Gleg, sharp-sighted.
Gleib, glebe = a portion of land.
Glowr, to stare.
Glunch, to frown.
Gowans, wild flowers.
Gowd, gold.
Gowk, a cuckoo = a fool.
Graip, a stable fork.
Grape, to grope.
Graith, dress or equipments.
Grat, past tense of greet.
Gree, to agree.
Greet, to shed tears.
Gruntle, the snout.
Grushie, a protruding muzzle.
Gude-willie, liberal hearted.
Gullie, a large knife.
Gumlie, muddy.
Gusty, tasteful, savoury.

Haet, a very small quantity.
Haffets, the temples.
Hafflins, nearly half-, not full-grown.
Haggis, a kind of pudding boiled in the stomach of a cow or sheep.
Hain, to save.
Hairst, harvest.
Hale, whole.
Hallan, a turf seat against a wall.
Haly, holy.
Han' durk, hand labour.
Hansel = hand-sale, first instalment of a bargain.
Hap, to wrap.

GLOSSARY.

Happer, hopper of a mill.
Harn, coarse linen.
Hash, a careless fellow.
Haslock, the wool on a sheep's neck.
Haughs, lowlands.
Hav'rel, half-witted.
Hawkie, a white-faced cow.
Hecht, promised.
Herryment, plundering.
Heugh, a pit.
Hilchan, limping.
Hind, a farm labourer.
Hirple, to walk lame, to limp.
Hissel, a flock.
Histie, dry, barren.
Hoast, host, a cough ; to cough.
Hoddan, jolting.
Hoddin, undyed wool.
Hog-shouther, to justle shoulders.
Hotch'd, topsy-turvy ; mixed.
Hool, outer skin or case.
Houghmagandie, fornication.
Howe-backet, hollow-backed.
Howe, hollow.
Howk, to dig.
Hoy, to urge.
Hoyte, to move clumsily.
Hunkers, the hams.
Hurdies, the buttocks.

Ilka, every.
Indentin, entering into an indenture.

Jad, jade.

Jauk, to idle.
Jaup, to splash.
Jing, a petty oath.
Jink, to turn suddenly.
Jinker, sprightly.
Jo, a sweetheart.
Jocteleg, a clasp-knife.
Jow, to swing as a bell.
Jundie, to justle.

Kail, cabbage, as in sea-kale.
Kane, kain, fowls, etc., paid as rent.
Kebars, rafters.
Kebbuck, cheese.
Keek, to peep.
Keilbaigie, whisky from Kilbaigie distillery.
Kiaugh, anxiety.
Kirn, a churn.
Kitchen, to give relish to.
Kittle, to tickle.
Kiutlin, to cuddle, to fondle.
Knaggie, knotty.
Knowe, a knowl = hillock.
Kyte, the belly.
Kythe, shown.

Lag, sluggish.
Laithfu', bashful.
Lallans, Lowland Scotch.
Lang-kail, cabbage cooked, but not cut up.
Lang-tocher'd, long = well dowered.
Lave, the leavings = remainder.

Laverock, a lark.
Lawin, a tavern score.
Lay, part of a weaver's loom.
Lea-rig, grassy ridge.
Lee, untilled land.
Lee-lang, life-long.
Leeze, blessing; leeze me on drink = blessings on drink.
Lift, the sky.
Limmer, a whore.
Link, to trip along.
Linn, a waterfall.
Lint, flax.
Lintwhite, linnet.
Loan, milking-shed.
Loof, the palm of the hand.
Loot, past of let.
Loun, a rogue.
Lowan, lowin, flaming.
Lug, the ear; "at the lug of," close to.
Luggies, a small wooden dish, with a handle.
Lum, a chimney.
Lunt, smoke.
Lyart, hoary.

Mae, more.
Mailen, mailin, a farm.
Mauken, a hare.
Meikle, much, a great quantity.
Melder, a load of corn for the mill.
Melvie, to soil with meal.
Mense, good manners.
Messan, a small dog.
Mill, a snuff-box.

Mim, prim.
Mirk, dark.
Moro, El Morro, a fort in Cuba.
Mottie, full of motes.
Moudewurt, a mole.
Muchkin, a pint.

Nappy, ale.
Nick, to cheat.
Nick, a notch, or wound.
Nieve, a fist.
Niffer, to barter.
Nit, a nut.
Nowt, black cattle.

Orra, superfluous.
Ou, wool.
Outler, cattle lying in the fields at night.
Owsen, oxen.

Paitrick, a partridge.
Pat, a pot.
Pechan, the stomach.
Petted, fretted.
Philibeg, the kilt.
Pickle, a small quantity.
Plackless, without a plack = penny.
Poind, to seize cattle for rent.
Poortith, poverty.
Powts, a poult, or chick.
Preen, a pin.
Prig, to haggle about a bargain.

Quean, a young woman.
Quey, a young cow.

GLOSSARY.

Raep, raip, or *rape,* a rope.
Raible, to rattle nonsense.
Rair, to roar.
Raize, to rouse.
Randie, a sturdy beggar.
Rash-buss, a bush of rushes.
Raucle, reckless.
Rax, to rack = stretch.
Ream, to froth.
Rede, counse
Reek, smoke.
Reestet, withered.
Riddle, instrument for sifting corn.
Riggin, the ridge of a house.
Rigwoodie, the rope, or chain traces; so lank and withered.
Ripp, a handful of corn.
Risk, to make a noise like tearing roots from the ground.
Rive, to tear.
Roon, a shred, the selvage of woollen cloth.
Row, to roll.
Rowt, to low.
Rung, a cudgel.
Runkle, winkle.
Runt, the stalk of cabbage.
Ryke, to reach.

Sair, to serve.
Sark, a shirt or shift.
Saugh, a willow.
Saumont, salmon.
Scaith, to harm.
Scaur, a precipitous bank.
Sconner, a loathing, to loathe.

Screed, a rent.
Scrieve, to move rapidly.
Scrimply, scarcely.
Shaird, shard; a shred.
Shavie, to do an ill turn.
Sheugh, a trench.
Shor'd, threatened.
Shot right kettle, a difficult or perilous shot.
Sinsyne, since that time.
Skaith, to harm.
Skrigh, skittish.
Skellum, a good-for-nothing fellow.
Skelp, to strike.
Skelpit, to hurry.
Skirl, to shriek.
Sklent, aslant.
Skreigh, to scream.
Skyte, a smart stroke.
Slaps, a gap in a hedge.
Slypet, slipped, fell over.
Smeek, smoke.
Smoor, to smother.
Smytrie, a collection of small creatures.
Snash, abusive language.
Sned, to lop off.
Snecshin, snuff.
Snell, bitter.
Snick, a latch.
Snick-drawing, over-reaching.
Snirtle, to sniff.
Snood, a ribbon for the hair.
Snool, to keep under.
Snoove, to sneak away.
Snowk, to snuff, as a dog.

Sowens, oatmeal drink.
Sonsie, lucky.
Souter, a shoe-maker.
Sowther, to solder.
Spavie, the spavin.
Spean, to wean.
Speat, a sudden flood in a river.
Speel, to climb.
Speels, to climb.
Spence, the parlour.
Spier, to ask a question.
Splore, noisy merriment.
Sprittie, spirited.
Spunkies, sparks, will-o'-the-wisp.
Spurtle, a stick to stir porridge.
Stacher, to stagger.
Stank, a stagnant pool.
Stark, stout.
Staumrel, half-witted.
Staw, stole.
Steek, to shut, a stitch.
Steer, to trouble.
Steeve, firm.
Stech, or *stegh*, to cram.
Sten'd, to rear as a horse.
Stent, a task.
Sterling, a silver coin.
Stey, steep.
Stibble-rig, stibble = stubble; stibble-rig, the reaper who takes the lead in harvest.
Stick-an-stowe, completely.
Stimpart, a quarter of a peck.
Stinted, stunted.
Stock, a plant of colewort, cabbage.

Stoor, sounding hollow, hoarse.
Stoure, dust.
Stownlins, stealthily.
Stowp, a jug.
Stroan, to spout.
Strunt, spirituous liquor.
Studdie, an anvil.
Sturtan, frightened.
Styme, a glimpse.
Sucker, sugar.
Sugh, a sigh.
Swank, limber.
Swankie, an agile lad or lass.
Swatch, a sample.
Swats, small-beer.
Syne, since.

Tackets, shoe-nails.
Tap-pickle, grain at the top of the stalk.
Tapsalteerie, topsy-turvy.
Tassie, a cup.
Tawie, tame.
Tawted, uncombed.
Tent, to attend, a field pulpit.
Tentie, cautiously.
Tentless, carelessly.
Teugh, tough.
Thack, thatch.
Thack an' raep = in order, denoting what is well regulated.
Thairm, catgut for a fiddle.
Thole, to bear.
Thowe, to thaw.
Thrung, busy.
Threap, to assert.

Through, "to mak' to through," to make good.
Thrissle, a thistle.
Timmer, timber.
Tine, to lose, or suffer loss.
Tirl, to tap gently.
Tittle, to whisper.
Tocher, marriage-portion.
Toom, empty.
Tow, a rope.
Towmond, towmont, a twelvemonth.
Tozie, towzie, rough.
Toyte, to totter.
Trepan, to steal or kidnap.
Tryste, an appointment.
Tulzie, a fight.
Twine, to deprive.

Uncos, news.
Usquebae, whisky.

Vauntie, joyous.
Virls, ferule = a ring.

Wad, a bet.
Waesucks! alas!
Wale, to choose.
Walie, large.
Wame, womb = the belly.
Wark-lume, a working-tool.
Warlocks, a wizard.
Warl', the world.
Warly, worldly.
Warstle, to wrestle.

Waught, a draught,
Wauket, callous.
Waur, worse.
Waur't, worst.
Wawlie, strapping.
Wean, a child.
Wechts, scales for weighing.
Wheep, small-beer.
Whaizle, to wheeze.
Whid, to run about.
Whigmeleeries, whims.
Whins, furze.
Whissle, to change money.
Whittle, a knife.
Whun-stane, whinstone = trap, or other hard rock.
Wiel, a small whirlpool.
Wimplin, to curl.
Winn, to winnow.
Win't, winded.
Winnock-bunker, a window-seat.
Wintle, a staggering motion.
Winze, to swear.
Wonner, to wonder.
Won, to dwell.
Woodie, a halter for the gallows.
Wooer-babs, garters knotted below the knees.
Wud, mad.
Wyte, to reproach.

Yealins, yearlings = of the same age.
Yill-caup, ale-cup.
Yird, earth.

www.ingramcontent.com/pod-product-compliance
Lightning Source LLC
Chambersburg PA
CBHW031959230426
43672CB00010B/2205